FROM A ROCK
TO A HARD PLACE

FROM A ROCK
TO A HARD PLACE

THE STORY OF
JEAN CLARK ZWOLIŃSKA MBE

Dale Vargas

© Copyright 2008 Dale Vargas

First Published 2008 by Dale Vargas

ISBN: 978-0-9559201-0-3

Design by Mousemat Design Ltd

Printed in the UK by MRT
www.mrtresponse.com

Contents

Introduction

IT IS ABOUT 7 AM and just getting light when a silver-haired elderly lady, upright and strong for her 86 years emerges from her apartment in a house in the eastern suburbs of Warsaw to go to the market some 100 metres from her front door. She walks with a slight limp and the help of a single crutch after a hip replacement with some complications a few years ago.

"*Dzień dobry, Pani Nowicka*", she greets an acquaintance in an accent more often heard on Princes Street Edinburgh than Grochowska. She knows most of the residents in the area for she has lived here for sixty years. It is a pleasant street – or would be if they would repair the plaster and paint the woodwork of the handsome well proportioned three- and four-storeyed houses that still bear the evidence of shells from World War II.

An hour later she will be back carrying her shopping to her comfortable two-roomed apartment on the ground floor. Her elder daughter may call on her sometime during the day or maybe one of her two Polish grandchildren but these will be fleeting visits; more likely the day will include a phone call and maybe a meeting with one of her two remaining friends from the 'bad times' Betty and Hela, but she is alone a lot now. Her husband Jan died ten years ago after she had nursed him through the appalling effects of Alzeimer's disease. And her younger daughter has been in England with a family of her own for over thirty years now.

She reads a lot, a habit formed in early life, common to many 'lighthouse children'. The days are long but she has an extraordinary life to reflect upon: an unusual but happy childhood; a fairytale romance, followed by a period of extreme hardship, gradually easing into a comfortable old age – punctuated by events of great satisfaction.

Her father, who was a huge influence in her life, once told her, "You are on this earth to do things for other people." She has lived her life by those standards: a life of service to family, friends, colleagues and complete strangers. That is why it has given me great pleasure to try to tell the story of the life of Jean Clark Zwolińska MBE.

Notes: Most of the Scottish women that married Poles called them by their English names: John, Stanley, Teddy etc. Throughout this story, I shall refer to Jean's husband as 'Jan' although Jean called him 'John' all his life, partly because it will avoid confusion with Jean's father – and partly because it was his name!

MBE is a Member of the Order of the British Empire, "awarded for outstanding service to the community that merits public recognition".

Acknowledgements

To put the story in its historical context, I have quoted freely from *The Heart of Europe, A Short History of Poland*, 1984, and *God's Playground, History of Poland*, 2005, both by Norman Davies. I have also quoted from an article by Mike Grundon in the *Shetland Times*, from *A Quiet Life* by Martha Robertson, and from an article by Margaret Peat in the *Scottish Magazine* of May 1991.

I am grateful to the following for their personal reminiscences and specialist local knowledge: my wife Krysia and her sister Wanda; Ian Clark, Jean's brother; Merle Frames, Jean's niece; Gwen Hughes and Jennifer Stewart, Ada Sieczkowska's sister and niece; Ronnie MacLean, formerly of Tobermory; Shuggy MacAlister of Tobermory; Karin Schouten of Stornaway; Barbara Bruce of Boddam; Marion Scollay, Curator of the Heritage Centre, Bressay; Ian Chalmers, former Cultural Secretary at the British Embassy in Warsaw; Betty Skwarek and Hela Boryń, Jean's friends in Warsaw; Sarah Riley, Second Secretary, Rebecca Claxton, Personal Assistant to Deputy Head of Mission and Witek Opertowski, Embassy Driver, all of the British Embassy in Warsaw.

I am also grateful to Kirsty Shanahan and Robert Dudley for their help and advice with the text. Of course, any errors are mine alone.

Reproduced photographs are of Rhubha nan Gall by Peter J Clarke (cover) and of Muckle Flugga by Philip Plisson (colour section).

1
Childhood: Ailsa Craig & Bressay

THERE CANNOT BE MANY PEOPLE holding a birth certificate showing their birthplace as Ailsa Craig, Ayrshire, Scotland. Jean Craig Stewart Clark was born there in 1921 (her second name reflecting that fact), the fourth child and third daughter of John and Isabella Clark. Her father was a lighthouse keeper and the families lived in the home station on the island.

John Clark had been born in 1886 and was brought up in Glasgow, where his father was a sergeant in the City Police. John worked first in coastal shipping, was a policeman in Oban, and then a seaman on the lightship *Hesperus*, based at Oban. He was appointed a keeper in January 1914.

Jean's mother, Isabella, born in 1889, was the daughter of Adam and Elizabeth Bennett; her father had been a superintendent engineer with Babcock & Wilcox, responsible for the installation of steam boilers in the woollen mills around Alva at the foot of the Ochils. He was also organist in the United Free Church of Scotland. John and Isabella Clark were married in February 1914.

Prior to Jean's arrival, John Clark had served at Sanda where Bessie was born in 1914 and Lena followed in 1917. The family moved to Ailsa Craig in 1917, where Bert was born in 1918 and Jean in 1921.

John Clark was a Scot and a Victorian; he could therefore be expected to have been a dour disciplinarian, careful with his money and disapproving of the joys of life. In fact he was none of these things: in line with the ethos of lighthouse keepers in general, his was a life of service and the idea of service to other people was passed on to his children, of whom all three girls became nurses

John Clark, Jean's father, as a Freemason

and one of the boys a policeman. As a product of the Scottish educational system he had been well educated in the context of the day and his brief experience in the Navy had taught him self-sufficiency and a good grounding in practical skills – essential for life as a lighthouse keeper. He was also enterprising, and one of his achievements had been to invent collapsible splints. He was not religious although he lived by a strong moral code, but he was a Freemason. Above all, he was a devoted father, setting his children clear lines but with a light touch.

John Clark was the life and soul of any party: he could sing, played at least three musical instruments well, was an excellent dancer, and was a very cheerful, genial character who took part in everything. Needless to say a man like this was popular with the ladies – a fact that was not lost on his wife. On more than one occasion she is said to have told him, "You can go if you wish, but you'll have to take five children with you".

Of course money was tight. A lighthouse keeper was not richly rewarded, although the job was secure, and he had a wife and five children to feed, but, as we shall see, opportunities for spending were limited too.

With father away for much of the time on lighthouse duty, much of the responsibility for bringing up the children fell on mother. Isabella was an altogether more dour character: her first reaction to a request was to say 'no' rather than 'yes' but she brought up the children well and, with five of them in sometimes primitive conditions, that is a great credit to her. One has to remember there were no washing machines or any of the modern kitchen gadgets, and the equivalent of dropping down to Tesco's involved at least a boat trip. Most home stations were in remote places and families relied on their small holdings for produce: vegetables in season; goats and chickens for milk and eggs - and meat; fish from fishermen or caught locally; often rabbits and sea birds. There was much work to be done before all these birds and animals were ready for the table.

Isabella was a strong woman – perhaps lacking the charisma

1922; Jean, aged six months, with her mother; in front are Lena, Bessie and Bert

of her husband and certainly in his shadow – but what Jean would describe as "a good soul." After John's death, she made her first trip by aeroplane to Warsaw – at the age of 82.

Ailsa Craig, in the Firth of Clyde, is a well known landmark to those travelling up the west coast of Ayrshire or playing golf at Turnberry. It is an inhospitable island rising abruptly from the sea to an elevation of 1,110 feet. It has a conical summit with very steep slopes except on the north-east side where it inclines more gently and it is possible to make a landing by boat. The lighthouse, designed by Thomas and David Stevenson, was completed in 1886; it had an oil-burning light that remained in use until 1911, when it was converted to incandescent. Siren fog signals were erected on the North and South ends of the island. They were removed in 1966 and replaced by a Tyfon fog signal, which gave three blasts, each of three seconds duration, every 45 seconds. This fog signal was discontinued in 1987.

The only other human activity on Ailsa Craig was quarrying for granite. Indeed the rock became famous for its curling stones. Quarrying has stopped there now, but there are still enough pieces of granite lying loose for a good number more stones yet. It was from Ailsa Craig granite that the curling stones used by the Scottish women's curling team, Winter Olympic gold medal winners in 2002, were made.

When Jean was a few months old, her father was posted to Bressay lighthouse at Lerwick on the Shetland Isles and the family moved there. The Shetlands are twelve hours on the ferry north from Aberdeen so this move transported them to a distant and isolated new world. Of course, Jean has no recollection of Ailsa Craig or Bressay but the family returned to the Shetlands some years later and we shall learn more about life there then.

xxx

Sixty years on, it is difficult to imagine just how distant and isolated Shetland must have been. Now it is only a few minutes by plane from the Scottish mainland and the character of the islands has been transformed by the discovery of oil in the North Sea in 1972. A huge oil terminal was built at Sullen Voe, bringing wealth and employment. The interests of the islanders have been well looked after in this respect: Shetland Island Council secured an Act of Parliament to ensure that the islanders benefited from a percentage of the value of the oil landed there. Several charitable trusts were created to provide facilities previously not available such as care homes for the elderly and leisure centres. Oil revenue also provided improved roads, schools and ferry services and the oil industry is now the islands' largest employer.

The main town, Lerwick, now a thoroughly international port with deep sea berthing and 3200 metres of quay, has retained much of its former charm. In addition to the ferries to Orkney, Aberdeen and some of the off-shore islands, there are still plenty of fishing boats, and the regattas ensure that there are plenty of sailing folk around in the summer.

Be that as it may, the Shetlanders are a distinct race from their Scottish cousins and proud of the fact. The Icelandic name of the Aberdeen ferry, the MV Hjaltland is the first hint of something different. The Shetlanders have their own dialect: mainly Lowland Scottish but with strong Scandinavian influences and to a lesser extent, Dutch and German. Indeed the Norwegian influence is plain to hear with some Norwegian words in the language as well as many place names. It is impossible for an 'incomer' to understand a conversation between two Shetlanders speaking in their dialect.

The Shetlanders' long and strong boating traditions have meant that they have always been much in demand by the navy, both merchant and military: many tales survive of caves where Shetlanders hid to escape the 'press gangs'. Their losses at sea were disproportionally high in both the world wars. They are also a very musical race with many more children learning instruments – fiddle and accordion are the most popular – than in the rest of Britain.

The island of Bressay, seven miles long and three wide, provides a natural protection for Lerwick harbour on the east side and can now be reached by a short ferry ride from Lerwick. The 53-foot tower of Bressay lighthouse on Kirkabister Ness guards the southern mouth of Lerwick harbour; indeed 'incomers' from England and Scotland are sometimes known as "South Mouthers", referring to their mode of entry rather than their speech.

Like all Shetland, Bressay is treeless and what scrub there is is kept to a minimum by sheep, which graze all over the island. The ground is mostly peat, used by the islanders for fuel amongst other things. It is dotted with croft houses but the habitation is still sparse. There is a shop and a currently rather unwelcoming hotel. The dominant feature of Bressay and the adjacent island Noss, a nature reserve, is the abundant and spectacular bird life: puffins, guillimots, gannets, skuas and shags all provide a magnificent display nesting on the cliffs and fishing at sea. There are also plenty of grey and common seals.

David and Thomas Stevenson engineered the light, which was built by the firm of Alex Wilson and first lit in August 1858. The light, two white flashes every 20 seconds, is visible for up to 23 nautical miles. In 1967 it was converted to electric operation and now has a sealed beam light. The foghorn (two blasts every 90 seconds) was very much a part of Lerwick life in foggy conditions until it was discontinued in 1987, when the station was fully automated and the keepers finally left.

Like Ailsa Craig, the lighthouse families on Bressay lived in accommodation next to the lighthouse. As usual there was a fair-sized piece of ground attached, enclosed by a white painted stone wall. This provided grazing space as well as a kitchen garden and play area for the children. In almost all lighthouse locations it would have been very dangerous for young children to leave the

Kirkabister Ness lighthouse, Isle of Bressay, Shetland

precinct unaccompanied.

Bessie enrolled at Bressay Public School – now Primary School – in September 1921, Lena the following April, and Bert later following his sixth birthday. Jean was still a baby. It was a two and a half mile walk from the lighthouse. According to Marion Scollay, born and bred on the island and now Curator of the Bressay Heritage Centre, the lighthouse families were much liked. Because of their access to boats, having a landing platform just below the lighthouse, they were unfailingly kind in providing assistance to the islanders. Marion described it as a "lichtsome", meaning "happy" relationship. "It was a sad day for the people of Bressay when the lighthouse was automated". The keepers' cottages are now let out for self-catering accommodation and there are plans for a visitor centre.

2
The Lighthouse Service

I AM GRATEFUL TO JEAN'S brother, Ian Clark, for this explanation of how the Lighthouse Service used to work.

"On walking along George Street Edinburgh you see the miniature lighthouse above the entrance to No. 84. This is the Head Quarters of the Northern Lighthouse Board, commonly known as the NLB. This public body is responsible for the lighting and buoying of the coast of Scotland and the Isle of Man. It liaises with Trinity House which is responsible for England, Wales, the Channel Islands and Gibraltar and the Irish Lighthouse Authority which covers the Irish coast, north and south. The NLB is governed by a Board of Commissioners consisting of several full-time members plus Sheriffs and Lords Provost of Scotland.

"Nowadays all the lighthouses are automatic, but in my day each lighthouse was inspected every three years by a posse of these gentlemen who arrived on the lighthouse tender, *Pharos*. The arrival in white plimsolls and yachting caps was a sight to behold! The lighthouse keepers turned out in their best uniform with everything spick and span for the inspection. We children looked on in amazement at these strange visitors from another world. Each child was given a small cardboard box of sugary sweets from some posh shop in Edinburgh. They obviously knew the number of children at each station for, in spite of our machinations, we only managed to receive one box each.

"The first proper manned lighthouse in Scotland was lit

on 1 December 1787 at Kinnaird Head, Fraserborough. The first keeper was James Park, a retired sea captain. He was employed at a wage of one shilling per night plus free lodging "on condition that each night he has another person with him, whom he is to instruct in the manner of cleaning the lantern and cleaning and lighting the lamps". In addition to his wage and shelter he was provided with pasture for one cow. The first lighthouse to be fully automatic was Fidra in 1970 and the last was Fair Isle South on 31 March 1998. Lighthouses remain but, after 200 years, a way of life has gone.

"I must mention the Stevenson family who, from 1804 to 1939, were the engineers responsible for building and maintaining the lighthouses for NLB. First was Robert who achieved worldwide fame for the construction of Bell Rock lighthouse. I mention them because they controlled the way in which the conditions and attitude to life in the service developed. Their attitude to dedicated work, morals and welfare prevailed to the end. They required the keepers to be self-disciplined, patient and calm under pressure. In return they were paid a reasonable regular wage, paid no local taxes, and were provided with free housing, lighting and heating. All household articles and furniture were provided at each house. Bedding was a personal issue and moved with them. Discipline was strict and dismissal not uncommon. Promotion was by seniority leading to a reasonable pension at age 65.

"The recruitment of lighthouse keepers really targeted three groups: (i) Preferred were the sons of lighthouse keepers whom the authorities knew from birth and who had grown up as children in the service; (ii) Seamen, for obvious reasons; and (iii) Tradesmen; by that I mean blacksmiths, carpenters, bricklayers, etc.

"Welfare was an important feature of the service with free medical care for all the family. Attention was paid to the children's education by postings to 'school stations'. These were stations where schools were reasonably accessible –

although of course 'reasonable' is relative to the context. Prior to the Education Act of 1944, so-called 'missionaries' visited stations to encourage the teaching of the 3Rs. Boxes of library books were sent to all stations plus the weekly *Scotsman* and the *Illustrated London News,* which was passed round groups of stations.

"For the wives it was a hard life but not an unpleasant one. Take my mother's case. Having been brought up in Glasgow she was used to gas lighting, flush toilet, handy shops and medical attention. On marrying she started at Sanda, a small island off the South coast of the Mull of Kintyre. Within a year her first child was born. In such a case other wives rallied round in support. Similarly they all helped in case of sickness. This became a way of life and, while isolated, it was never lonely. In almost all cases drinking water was carried from a well and washing water from water tanks which collected storm water. In all stations there was a pecking order according to the husbands' seniority. There being one wash house with a coal fire boiler, the principal keeper's wife washed on Mondays, then each wife in descending order. Water management being important, it followed that wash day was also bath day, namely in a tin tub. After the washing had been scrubbed it was hung out hoping it would not be blown away. Cooking was done on a kitchen coal fire range, black leaded every day, frying on a primus. There only being paraffin lamps, a Tilly lamp was considered the height of luxury. The ordering and carrying of supplies had to be thought out well ahead and a reserve of supplies kept in case of bad weather. At fog signal stations with engines, each year the district superintendent with two officials attended to carry out the maintenance. They were lodged and fed in the keepers' homes, pecking order again laid down so that the Superintendent stayed with the Principal Keeper and so on.

"The lighthouse keepers' basic duty was to watch over the light during the hours of darkness and to ensure that it

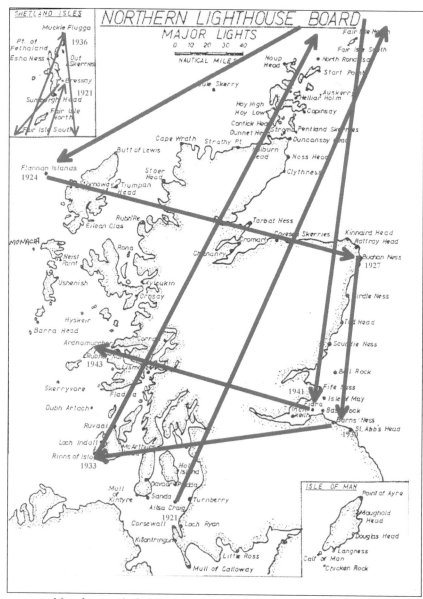

Map showing the lighthouses at which the Clark family were stationed

was burning bright and clear. Keeping the outside of a lantern clear in a blizzard while hanging from the grab rail with one hand was no joke. No reading, writing or handicraft work was permitted in the light room during watches. Was the rule obeyed? I think not, as who was there to check? To fall asleep meant instant dismissal. At isolated stations, in the event of a long spell of fog or sickness, it was not unknown for wives to assist with the watches, especially when bad weather prevented help from arriving. The keepers were also responsible for the maintenance of the station houses and grounds and the whitewashing of all the buildings. Pre-war, there were over 90 manned lighthouses, manned by several hundred men. The last lighthouse keeper was recruited in 1981 and the last retired in 1998."

The nine lighthouses at which John Clark was keeper during Jean's time in Scotland were built between 1819 (Buchan Ness) and 1901 (Barns Ness). The lighthouses were administered by the Commissioners of Northern Lighthouses. Their construction was usually in response to requests from local magistrates, town councils, harbour trustees, Lloyds the insurers or the Scottish Shipmasters Association. Approval was required from the Board of Trade and Trinity House. The design and construction was the responsibility of the Engineers to the Commissioners who, during this period, appear to have been entirely staffed by three generations of the Stevenson family, mentioned above: Robert (1772-1850), Robert's sons Alan (1807-1865), David (1815-1886) and Thomas (1818-1887), and David's sons David Alan (1854-1938) and Charles (1855-1950). Robert alone was responsible for no fewer than fifteen of Scotland's lighthouses. The author Robert Louis Stevenson was Thomas's son and there have been various suggestions as to which island gave him the original idea for his novel *Treasure Island*.

The early lights were mantel and paraffin, but the engineers were constantly looking for ways of improving them: dioptic lenses, incandescent bulbs, revolving, flashing, and group flashing lights and finally automatic. There were also various fog signals, foghorns and sirens.

The working conditions for the keepers varied considerably from light to light: most lighthouses were isolated but some were more isolated than others. On Ailsa Craig, which was completely uninhabited except for the Quarry Company, there were three keepers living with their families at the home station. Each keeper would do three months of duty at a time followed by one month off. Until wireless telephone communications were established in 1935, the light keepers used to depend on pigeons for the conveyance of messages. If a doctor or supplies were required urgently in stormy weather, when it was impossible to have messages taken by carrier pigeon, a system of signals by fire was used. One fire on the castle path showing the lighthouse to the North indicated "bring doctor for lighthouse"; two fires on the castle path (one at the same place as the lighthouse fire, and the other 20–30 yards above it) meant "bring doctor for Quarry Company"; one fire at the north end of the Castle Flat showing the lighthouse to the South indicated that provisions were required.

At Muckle Flugga, there were three light keepers on the rock at any one time, each of the keepers manning the station spending six weeks on and two weeks ashore. Conditions were primitive: when a new dwelling block was built in 1968 in space saved by electrification, it replaced conditions where "light keepers slept in a crows nest and ate in a cell". Fresh water and any heavy stores were landed at the rock by boat but reliefs were sometimes long overdue because of heavy seas which made a landing impossible. The introduction of helicopters which made trips to the lighthouse once every two weeks greatly eased the keepers' lot.

3

Flannan Isles & Buchan Ness

I<small>N</small> 1924, <small>WHEN</small> J<small>EAN WAS</small> 3 and the elder children 9, 7 and 6, John Clark was appointed to be one of the keepers at the Flannan Isles lighthouse, twenty-one miles northwest of the Island of Lewis in the Outer Hebrides

The Flannan Isles lie in an area known as the Atlantic Outliers. This uninhabited archipelago of seven main islands, with about 45 rocks and islets, is sometimes known as 'The Seven Hunters'. In 1549 Dan Munro called them the 'Seven Haly Isles'. He said they were inhabited only with "infinit wylde sheep" that "cannot be eaten by honest men but make good tallow". The Bernera crofters still bring their sheep out to the islands to graze because of the high quality of the grass.

Before the Flannan Isles lighthouse was built, The Seven Hunters were a hazardous group of isles so named for destroying ships on their way to Scottish ports. The lighthouse, designed by David Alan and Charles Stevenson, was built on Eilean Mor, a major island of the group, in 1899. Eilean Mor is also known as "The Island of the Dead" – hardly an encouragement to a newly appointed keeper. The light is 330 feet above sea level and flashes white every 30 seconds. The Flannan Isles was what was termed a 'rock station' with four keepers, each keeper serving three months on the rock and one month ashore. The relief keeper was carried out each month by the lighthouse tender, *Hesperus*. In fact 'the Flannan' is not a sea-washed rock but a fair sized island, about 38 acres in area, where the keepers had constructed a mini-golf course. There are also the ruins of a corbelled sixth century building, St Flann's Chapel. This and the building beside it, possibly a dwelling, were described by the Ancient Monuments Commission as "bothies of the clan McPhail". People living on Uig still make an annual pilgrimage to the chapel.

The Flannan Isles lighthouse is most famous for 'the disappearance'. On 15 December 1900, it was noticed that the light had not been lit in the lighthouse, but bad weather prevented anyone getting to the island until 26 December. When the crew of the *Hesperus* finally arrived at the island, they found it deserted. The lamps were primed and ready for lighting; there was a diary entry made on the morning of 15 December that the lamp should be lit, but no signs of life. Explanations put forward have included a freak wave, and a terrible row in which two were killed and the murderer committed suicide – but no bodies were ever found. In spite of intensive investigations, the mystery has never been explained.

Superintendent Robert Muirhead in his official report for the NLI, wrote:

> "I am of the opinion that the most likely explanation of the disappearance of the three men is that they have all gone down on the afternoon of Saturday 15 December 1900 to the proximity of the west landing to secure the box with the mooring ropes etc. and that an unexpectedly large roller had come up on the island, and that a large body of water going up higher than where they were and coming down upon them, had swept them away with resistless force".

The tragedy was given an edge of mystery and romanticism by Wilfred Wilson Gibson's epic poem, *Flannan Isle* which tells the story of three men discovering the disappearance:

> O chill clutch on our breath –
> We thought how ill-chance came to all
> Who kept the Flannan Light

And how the rock had been the death
Of many a likely lad:
How six had come to a sudden end
And three had gone stark mad:
And one whom we'd all known as friend
Had leapt from the lantern one still night,
And fallen dead by the lighthouse wall:
And long we thought
On the three we sought,
And of what might yet befall.

Since the lighthouse was automated in 1971, the islands have become an increasingly important nesting place for sea birds, especially auks but including Leach's Petrel, for which they are one of only seven known nesting sites in Europe.

The families of the lighthouse keepers lived at the shore station, a handsome two-storey house at Breasclete on the mainland of Lewis. Ian Clark, the youngest of the family, was born in this house in 1926. Breasclete is a small hamlet, comprising a dozen or so crofts, and apart from a small factory by the pier producing health food supplements, it has probably changed little in the

Former Flannan Isles Shore Station, Breasclete, Isle of Lewis

last seventy years. It runs into Calanais, a similar settlement with some standing stones of archaeological significance and the luxury of a post office. Even now the islands of Lewis and Harris are something of a culture shock for foreigners – even mainland Scots. This is largely because of the prevalence of the Gaelic language, the crofting tradition and the constraining influence of the religious 'elders'. There is not much of 'clans and kilts' here but the Leodhachs are fiercely proud of their traditions and have strong religious affiliations – including the young people. The pervading brand of religion is the Free Church of Scotland, but there are also the Free Presbyterians, the High Church of Scotland, the Continuing Presbyterian Church and numerous break-away groups. These are popularly known as the 'Wee Frees'. The difference between these various sects seems to be personal rather than doctrinal. What they all share is an absolute belief in the words of the Bible, a strict code of conduct, especially in observance of the Sabbath, and a passionate dislike of Roman Catholicism. A recent attendance at a FPC service in Stornaway was a salutary experience. The Minister who spoke for 70 minutes in a rambling, humourless monologue on a passage from the Acts of the Apostles, had four swipes at "Popery" and its "nonsense and superstitions". The congregation also prayed to be "saved from the evils of Rome and Islam". Although the Clark family was not particularly religious, they did take their children to Church and/or Sunday School. At Breasclete it would have been of the Wee Free variety and it is very likely that the elder children were influenced by it. This would explain Bessie's reaction to Jean's proposed marriage some years later.

xxx

In 1927 the family was on the move again, this time to Buchan Ness near Peterhead on the east coast. Before the lighthouse was built, shipwrecks were common on this stretch of the coast. Between November 1816 and March 1819, 20 ships were wrecked including the sloop *Marchioness of Huntly* at Boddam itself in 1817. Surveys began for a lighthouse in 1819. Buchan Ness, the most easterly point on the Scottish mainland, near the village of Boddam, was decided upon, but it took eight years before it was complete. Robert Stevenson was the engineer and John Gibb of Aberdeen the contractors. The 114 feet high lighthouse tower, to which red bands were added in 1907 to distinguish it as a day mark, like all lighthouses is a sturdy construction. It was put to the test in an unexpected way during the Second World War when it was hit by drifting mines – twice. No one was injured and the material damage consisted of three lantern panes cracked and 12 other glass panes broken in the tower. More damage was done to the keepers' houses, where the ceilings of the kitchen and one bedroom of the First Assistant's house were brought down by the explosion.

There have been many changes to the light since 1827: in 1910 it was the first lighthouse to have a dioptric (flashing light); in 1978, it was converted to electric operation. It was automated in 1988 and the foghorn, added in 1904, was discontinued in 2000.

Buchan Ness was a three keeper station. When the fog signal was running, one keeper was on watch in the light room, one in the engine room and one was off watch. As on most shore stations, the families lived in accommodation in the lighthouse complex, a number of single storey buildings, painted white with the window surrounds picked out in a different colour – one of the NLB signatures – and there were the usual outbuildings: store room, engine room, workshop and washing block. The complex, covering an acre or so and surrounded by a stone wall that was kept whitewashed by the keepers, is typical of NLB shore stations. It covered the surface of what is actually an island, although it is only separated from the shore by a ravine. In the 1920s there was a bridge connecting the island to the mainland; this has since been replaced by a causeway of no more than 20 yards.

The proximity of the lighthouse to the fishing village of Boddam made this a suitable posting for a keeper with a family, four of whom were of school age, although on occasions in the past it had proved to be their undoing: at least two lighthouse keepers were relieved of their duties for spending too long in the village pub. Boddam, just south of Peterhead, is a fishing village built mostly of attractive brown stone buildings; the small harbour with massive concrete walls lies a hundred yards or so up the coast from the lighthouse.

When the Clark family arrived in 1927, the fishing was already in decline. A newspaper article of 1928 read, "Nowhere however is the decline of the North East fishing villages more pronounced, or the disasters more acute, than at Boddam. There are now only a dozen boats, most of them with motor engines and no curing is done at all." In 1930 there was the lament, "Built half a century ago or more to accommodate the fleet of ships that filled it, the harbour is now silent and deserted with grass growing on its piers". The advent of the trawler and the proximity of Peterhead, "where all fishing has been concentrated and whither many of the young and more energetic fishermen have migrated," were blamed. Now the fishing has been reduced to small catches of crab and lobster (to be exported to Spain!), but there is a fish-processing plant by the harbour. Although there has been quite a bit of building in recent years, most of the employment is at the nearby power station or in Peterhead, itself a rundown-looking town.

In 1927, Bessie was 12, Lena 10, Bert 9, Jean 6 and Ian 1,

Buchan Ness lighthouse with the village of Boddam behind

so Bessie went off to the secondary school in Peterhead – a bus journey away, while Lena, Bert and Jean attended the local primary school in Boddam, an easy walk from the lighthouse. Barbara Bruce has lived in the village all her life and, now a widow in her eighties, has fond memories of the lighthouse children, many of whom became good friends. She was too young to remember the Clark family but her elder sister Lal struck up a friendship with Bessie and used to visit her when, in later years, Bessie lived in Musselbrough. Barbara recalls many happy times over at the lighthouse where the children used to play rounders on the grass. Two other memories stick in her mind: first, how the coal for the lighthouse was delivered by ship which anchored off shore, lowered into a small boat, rowed to the harbour and then finally delivered by horse and cart. And second, how the keepers used to paint the lighthouse suspended in a bo'sun's chair. Nowadays scaffolding is used and it takes weeks.

Although Buchan Ness is a shore station it is not safe from the scourge of bad weather: it is in fact the most easterly point on the Scottish mainland. The combination of a high tide and a strong south easterly wind can produce a 'doubler'. On several occasions over the years a 'doubler' has crashed over the rocks, burst through the perimeter wall and flooded the houses.

After automation in 1988, the accommodation was sold. In 2000 it came up for sale again. The estate agent's notice read:

"The lighthouse at Buchan Ness, a rocky outcrop on the Aberdeenshire coast south of Peterhead, is one of the more unusual homes for sale at the moment. Accessed by a bridge which is under water at high tide and with its own helicopter pad, it is frequently battered by strong winds from the North Sea. And when there is a thick mist, the foghorn sounds to warn off ships out at sea. The unique property has given rise to a lot of interest in spite of the price tag of £200,000."

It was not sold. However the cottages now appear to be occupied and a further bungalow in a modern style, sadly not blending well with its surroundings, has been added.

4
Barns Ness & Islay

IN 1930 THE FAMILY MOVED to Barns Ness near Dunbar. This was a
'two-man station' where the keeper kept watch during the hours
of darkness. Barns Ness was considered a good posting because
a mile away was the old A1 road and a bus into Dunbar. It was a
rule at all stations that during the hours of daylight only one man
could be off site, but at least civilisation was not far away.

The lighthouse at Barns Ness is a 121 foot tower, made of
stone from Craigree (near Cramond) and Barnton quarries. The
stone has proved to be tough, as Barns Ness was machine gunned
during the War and no damage was sustained. It was designed by
David Alan Stevenson and the light was first lit in 1901.

The lighthouse had an old mantel and paraffin-operated light
but when it was converted to semi-automatic operation in 1966,
the manning was reduced to one. The sealed beam light, powered
by mains electricity had 1,300k candlepower and was the first of
its type to be used in the Commissioners' Service.

The keepers' accommodation was in houses next to the
lighthouse. These were the single storey whitewashed little
cottages that are a feature of the Northern Lighthouse Board's
properties. Much has been written about the lighthouses themselves
but very little about the architecture of the associated buildings.
Functionality seems to have been the main design feature. Being
necessarily in exposed and isolated places, they had to be able
to withstand the roughest of winter weather. They also had to
provide for the needs of several families throughout the year. At
Barns Ness, water was pumped up from a well by a windmill but
this was a far more accessible site than anything the Clark family

had experienced hitherto. There was even a grocery van that came to deliver the shopping.

In the days before the power station to the south, the cement works to the north, and the caravan site on the approach road, this must have been a beautiful place – at least in summer. Just in front of the lighthouse, there is a large rocky foreshore, perfect for children to search for crabs and shellfish. There are beaches on either side and a glorious view across the Firth of Forth to Bass Rock. On the land side of the lighthouse are several acres of meadow full of wild flowers in summer: a mass of harebells, poppies and ragwort give a spectacular splash of colour.

Jean (9) and Ian (5) attended a two-teacher school at East

Jean (right) with Annie McCormack at Rhinns Point on Islay

Barns about a mile away, and Bert (12) travelled the half-hour journey by bus to the Secondary School in Dunbar. Jean joined him two years later. Bessie and Lena had left school and, like all lighthouse children, left home to find work: they both went into domestic service until they were old enough to start nursing.

It is a feature of lighthouses in general that, although they are always located near the sea – sometimes even surrounded by it – the nearby area is rarely suitable for swimming. Barns Ness was unusual in this respect: it was possible to paddle and swim in shallow water. It was in the sea there that Jean learned to swim.

Jean: "We waited for the tide to come in. Bessie said, "You'll never learn to swim until you get *onto* the water. Walk along on your knees." I did that and she was swimming in front of me when I went into this great big hole. The next thing I can remember I was lying in the sands. Apparently when I went into the hole and disappeared from view, she grabbed my hair – we didn't wear bathing caps in those days – and pulled me out. That was my first swimming lesson. I picked it up quite quickly after that."

"Bert used to gather whelks and put them in a bag. Then they were put on a train and sent to London, so I suppose he made himself a bit of pocket money. I used to earn a little from doing odd jobs about the house: polishing candlesticks and cleaning boots. For cleaning the brasses I got a penny a week. We also used to earn some pocket money in the summer by opening the gates to visitors to the sandy beach."

Ian: "At East Barns there was a farm with about a dozen farm cottages that employed 16 pairs of Clydesdale horses. We boys each adopted our own horse which we would ride out. There was also a blacksmith, with whom we were friendly. I loved watching him shoeing the horses and repairing the farm implements.

"At harvest time we used to have great fun playing hide-and-seek in the stooks of corn. There was a threshing machine, driven by a steam engine, which used to travel from farm to farm. We used to amuse ourselves by killing the rats and mice exposed by the thresher. The sandy grass area surrounding the lighthouse was overrun by rabbits and the local gamekeeper used to wander about with a gun and set snares to catch them. If we saw one in a trap we would set it free: fortunately he never caught us.

"One unusual incident I remember was on a foggy morning when a German ship ran aground about two miles east of the lighthouse. We had to go to school but at lunchtime a few of us went over the fields to visit the scene – which we had been forbidden to do. Needless to say we were late back and in trouble…

"Barns Ness was a very tall lighthouse as it was on low-lying ground and it was in the path of migrating birds at certain times of year. In the morning there were frequently loads of dead birds lying dead on the ground after flying into the lantern and breaking their necks.

"When I re-visited the area recently, Barns Ness was deserted; the school had a tree growing through the roof, all the farm buildings have gone and the rest were derelict. With the nuclear power station and cement works not far away, it was altogether a rather depressing sight.

"Towards the end of our time at Barns Ness, Bessie became very ill and was in hospital for a long time. Eventually they decided that she had rheumatic fever. At this point Dad got notice to move to Islay; Jean was due to move on to secondary school and Bert was old enough to start work so he started as an apprentice with Dudgeon's, the chemist in Leith; he later joined the Royal Army Medical Corps. Lena also left home to start nursing, so it was Mum and Dad, Jean and I and Bessie on a stretcher, as she still couldn't walk, that set off for Islay. We travelled by train to Oban, where we boarded the *Hesperus* for Islay. Just as we were about to cast off a steam valve blew in the engine room, frightening everyone out of their wits with the noise. It poured with rain all the way but the sea was calm and the rest of the journey was uneventful."

xxx

So, in 1933 it was on to Rhinns Point on Islay. Rhinns Point Lighthouse is situated on the small island of Orsay off the south coast of Islay. Rhinn is the Gaelic for point, but in this case the name comes from the Gaelic 'rann', a division. The Rhinns formed one of the three divisions of Islay. Orsay, owned by the NLB, sits across an inlet from the attractive fishing village of Portnahaven. The area is known for its striking expanse of Lewisian gneiss, the oldest rock in Europe.

Martha Robertson's father took over from John Clark as keeper at Rhinns. This description of life on the island is taken from her story, *A Quiet Life*.

"Orsay was a tiny green place, treeless and apparently devoid of interesting features. There were three little sandy beaches. Some way up from the pier was the usual 'park' (keepers' grounds) which contained the main garden and hen run. Another behind it contained a small ruined chapel in front of which stood a handsome Celtic cross. According to local legend St Columba had landed on Orsay from Ireland and built the wee chapel intending to use it as a base before later deciding to move further north to settle in Iona. The Rhinns suffered from a great deal of thick impenetrable fog.

"When the weather allowed there were excursions over to the main island to the twin villages of Port Wemyss and Portnahaven which were separated by a few hundred yards of rough road. The houses of Portnahaven lay in two tiers round a harbour which, at the time I am speaking of, was occupied by only a few rowing boats and the occasional skiff. There was one hotel, a Post Officecum-general store and two other quaint shops that sold everything from a needle to an anchor. Port Wemyss had no harbour, only two shops and no Post Office. The two villages shared a hall, a school and two churches. The hall, school and one of the churches were sited at the apex of a triangle formed by two roads leading to the rest of Islay."

The Rhinns was a 'three-keeper station'. The lighthouse was built in 1825 under the direction of Robert Stevenson and John Gibb of Aberdeen were the contractors for the splendid tower. The engineer had to use considerable ingenuity to find a way of distinguishing one light from another. The result was a light, alternately stationary and revolving, producing a bright flash every 12 seconds, without those intervals of darkness which characterise other lights on the coast. He also included some innovations: porches on the balconies to give the keepers protection when leaving the lantern room in stormy weather. The cost of this lighthouse was between £8,000 and £9,000. In 1978 the light was changed to electric operation and

The journey from Islay to Burrafirth, Unst, Shetland.
Jean (centre), her mother (second left) and brother, Ian (extreme right)

this sealed beam light, mounted on a gearless revolving pedestal, proved a real step forward in lighthouse illumination. The light, being sealed in a vacuum, does not tarnish or deteriorate. The Rhinns of Islay lighthouse was automated in 1998.

When the Clark family arrived at the Rhinns, the principal keeper was Mr McCormack. He had four children: a girl who was away at teacher training college, a son waiting to join the lighthouse service, a second daughter about to start nursing and a third daughter, Annie, of Jean's age. Bessie recovered from her illness and in due course started nursing at Haddington. Jean went to school in Bowmore and she and Annie McCormack stayed in a hotel in Portnahaven from Monday to Friday, returning to the lighthouse for the weekend. Ian and the McCormack boy went by boat each day to Port Wemyss Primary, a two-teacher school, where most of the children spoke Gaelic as a first language. Bessie and Mr McCormack always spoke to each other in Gaelic.

Jean: "On Sunday afternoons the boatman took the two of us, Annie McCormack and me, over on the boat to Port Wemyss; he took Ian across to his school in Portnahaven every day. Annie and I stayed in the hotel, paid for by the NLB. The bus picked us up in the morning and we travelled for about an hour to Bowmore, a trip some twenty miles round Loch Indaal, picking up children all the way. I can remember Mr Winnard, the Headmaster. We used to have a cooked meal midday – I remember a horrible stew – and then we came home between 5 and 6 and had our supper at the hotel. We did our homework there and then we were free to roam about. There was a group of us but nobody was looking after us.

"There was this church in the village – it was the "wee free church" of Scotland, not the united free, and we used to go into it at night. The Minister would show us 'Hell', a mural showing us what was waiting for us: it was a bit frightening. This was my first taste of freedom from the family and a very happy time. We had to make our own entertainment. I remember the McCormack son, he played the bagpipes and Bessie and Mr McCormack used to act out mimes at the ceilhids. Dad taught me the sword dance and the highland fling; he played the fiddle and the banjo – and the piano.

"I never kept up with Annie but I heard that she went to University and then back to teach in Portnahaven.

"We used to keep chickens and goats on the island. One day a weasel or a stoat – I forget which – turned up and killed all the chickens. They don't know how it got there as there were no weasels on Orsay; it could have come on a boat or it could have come along the telephone wires. They set a trap for it and put it in a cage. Dad went to drown it in a trough of water but it got out of the cage and shot up his sleeve. There was quite a scuffle but I don't think it bit him."

And it was on Islay that Jean met her first boyfriend, Angus Mackechnie. She was not very forthcoming about him, but she did say that she later named all her dogs after him. I'm not sure how pleased Mr Mackechnie would have been had he known that!

Although the crossing from Orsay to Islay is only a few minutes' boat ride across the channel, the tide and currents can cause real problems. It is easy to see why: even in summer huge waves can be seen hitting the rocks and the heavy swell makes getting in and out of the boat a hazardous exercise. By this time, Jean was a strong swimmer, but she earned herself a firm ticking off from her father when one day she succeeded in swimming across. Once even a whale got caught out and headed up the channel.

Jean: "The boatman was taking us across in his boat as usual – it was a small rowing boat – when we suddenly saw this big whale – I think it was a herring whale – heading straight for us. It found its way past the boat but as it went by, the boatman, who was a bit simple, tried to hit the whale with his oar. We all shouted at him – with the slightest flick of its tail, the whale could have had us all in the water."

Ian: "The rowing boat was handled by a local man employed by the Lighthouse Service, which also supplied the boat. The trip across the sound was about half a mile, but it could be dangerous especially in the spring tides when the tide could run at 9 knots in full flood. When this was so, the boatman would creep up near the shore as far as possible and then row like mad to get across to the pier on Orsay. On one occasion, the regular boatman was unavailable and it was arranged that a relative, who was there on holiday, would take us across. He didn't understand the tide problem and instead of starting off creeping along the shore, set off straight across. As the tide began to sweep us towards the sea, Dad, who was waiting near the pier, was shouting and screaming at the unfortunate stand-in boatman. We made it, but the poor man was so exhausted that he had to come up to the house to lie down."

Apart from the chickens there were other supplements to the regular diet on Orsay as Martha Robertson explains:

"The Rhinns lay on the migratory lanes for many species of birds. During this season dozens – sometimes hundreds – of birds crashed into the lighthouse and were killed. These provided unexpected delicacies for the table.

"Fishing was good at the Rhinns too: in all but the worst weather we could catch lythe and podleys from the boat and, when we couldn't go out, we could fish from a promontory near the pier. Sometimes a lythe could weigh up to fourteen pounds, requiring quite an effort to bring it close and lift it into the boat. The lythe is a beautiful fish, the skin and scales a lovely reddish gold with fine markings. In the right season you could run into a shoal of mackerel. They would launch themselves in dozens onto the waiting lines and you could have filled the boat.

"There was another form of fishing at the Rhinns too: flounder fishing. These wily fish are experts at camouflage: when they sense danger they wriggle just under the sand and lie still, so it takes a practised eye to spot them. The trick is to drift above the sand waiting for the tell-tale puffs that give away the flounder's position; then a lunge with a long spear can spike the fish."

Ian: "The Rhinns was a very happy station where everyone got on well. Although I spent much time on my own, I was never lonely. I wandered all over the island and made my own entertainment such as carving little boats using feathers as sails. At low tide, I would search the pools for edible crabs. In the summer, when we often had family visitors, ceilidhs were organised. The keepers had their own boat which they used for fishing and visits to the mainland.

"All stores and paraffin were delivered by the *Hesperus* but coal was brought by a schooner once a year. When stores or coal were landed, a farmer from the main island would swim his horse across behind a boat. It then used to pull the cart kept on the island to transport the stores up to the lighthouse. The horse was usually on the island for two or three days but one morning there was no sign of it. The keepers telephoned the farmer in a state of concern but the farmer reported that the horse was back in its own field. It must have realised that the time to swim was at slack tide, or it would have been swept out to sea."

Footnote: Annie McCormack did indeed return to Islay; she taught at the village school and married a Mr Cooper, who ran the local post office. When Mr Cooper died, she left the school and took over the post office herself – not altogether successfully. She now lives in a care home in Bowmore.

5

Muckle Flugga

IN MARCH 1936, JOHN CLARK received orders to move to Muckle Flugga, a lighthouse off the north coast of Unst, Shetland. He negotiated with his replacement for the sale of their livestock and the family set off. They travelled on the *Hesperus* to Oban, then by train to Aberdeen, on to Lerwick on the *St Sunniva*; then on to Baltasound on the *Earl of Zetland*. From Baltasound they went by road to Burrafirth, the home station of Muckle Flugga. Jean was by now sixteen and rather than start again at yet another school she stayed at home for a year "learning to be a housewife".

Further north than St Petersburg in Russia and Cape Farewell in Greenland and the Alaskan Peninsula, Muckle Flugga is the most northerly point in the British Isles. Its nearest railway station is Bergen in Norway. In 1811 a hurricane storm sank the 98-gun *St George* and the 74-gun *Defence in the Baltic* with the loss of 2,000 lives, twice as many as died in the Battle of Trafalgar. After this the Admiralty felt that, as Royal Navy ships would be passing the Shetlands on their way to blockading Russia's northern ports, the unlit state of the coast was a clear danger that required action.

The location chosen for a lighthouse was a rock, 200 feet above sea level, a mile north of Unst and work began in 1854. In spite of its height above the sea, when the winter gales began to break over the rock, it soon became clear that the proposed 50 foot tower was not high enough. Waves invaded the living area and the Principal Keeper reported that 40 feet of stone dyke had been knocked down, six water casks carried away, and that "we had not a dry part to sit down in or even a dry bed to rest upon at night". A 64 foot high brick tower was then built with foundations sunk ten feet into the rock; it was the first lighthouse in such an exposed location to be built of brick; this was because all the building materials had to be transported by boat and bricks were easier than the traditional lumps of granite. The operation cost £32,000, a huge amount of money in those days. The lighthouse was first named 'North Unst' but changed in 1964 to 'Muckle Flugga'. The name comes from Old Norse, 'Mikla Flugey' meaning 'large steep-sided island'. A permanent light first appeared on 1 January 1858.

Muckle Flugga was generally considered to be the most unfriendly site in the United Kingdom. Photographs, in which it looks like a stubby little tower, with none of the grandeur of the magnificent obelisk lighthouses, give little impression of what it is like in reality. It was a 'four keeper station', three keepers being on the lighthouse at any one time and the fourth ashore.

This is an extract from an article written by Mike Grundon in the *Shetland Times* of February 1995, as the keepers were to leave Muckle Flugga for the last time:

"This is a place of extreme violence in one of the most inaccessible parts of Shetland. It was commonplace for 'green water' – not just spray – to sweep past the keepers' kitchen, 180 feet above sea level.

"The landing stage was built to the shape and line of the natural formations. A small iron ladder runs up out of the water to a narrow concrete path and railing which runs along the spine of a fin of the rock known as "the comb". The path then dives down a short causeway which crosses the head of a boulder strewn beach at the foot of the Flugga. Facing the new arrival is a flight of 250 steps up to the lighthouse.

"Everything had to brave this landing whether they were going in or coming out. If at the end of a month's duty the state of the sea was too bad on the day and time allocated for the changeover, the luckless keeper was abandoned until the next scheduled trip two weeks later. If at the end of that time the weather was again too poor, he was stuck for another two weeks and so on.

"All supplies had to be sent up a cable from the landing to

the top, hauled by a winch but loaded by hand. Until 1960 when several new buildings were erected to extend the living and service areas, everything was housed within the thick curving walls of the tower itself. At the bottom of the tower were the larders. Up a narrow iron ladder and through a hatch was the kitchen. The next floor was the bedroom where the three keepers slept in triple-decker bunks. Another ladder led to the machine room and watch room, where the work of the keepers was centred. The final steps led up to the business end of the whole complex: the light itself.

"Blazing away with 910k candlepower focussed out to the 25 mile horizon by twin hand-ground glass reflectors, it marks Great Britain's outer edge with a white double flash every 20 seconds. To the North, past the little rock outcrop known as Out Stack, there is no major landfall until you reach the Arctic – which is not land anyhow! It is incredible to think that four intelligent and motivated human beings should devote their lives to providing this service.

"Life on the rock is one of self-reliance. The keeper has to do everything from cooking his own meals to stripping and repairing a generator and painting the outside of the dome. The lack of entertainment was a problem too: reading, bird watching and woodwork were popular pastimes. It takes a certain mentality to be an offshore lighthouse keeper. All knew stories of colleagues who went through training and were taken out to their first posting only to go "stir-crazy" within days. The keepers had to be able to live together without quarrels and to be at peace with themselves. To find these qualities in a man who was an able and improvisational engineer, not worried about being separated from family and friends and civilization, must have been difficult.

"Sailors the world over owe their safe passage to the silent lighthouse keepers. That should be remembered with gratitude."

The shore station at Burra Firth, where the lighthouse tending boat, the *Grace Darling,* along with a boatman, was based, has now been taken over by Scottish National Heritage as a visitor centre with a resident warden for the Herma Ness Nature Reserve. Unst is the most northerly of the three main Shetland islands and travellers from Lerwick must still take two ferries to get there. For a while, commercial flights used an airport at Baltasound, but these ceased when the RAF recently vacated their radar station at Saxa Vord. It remains one of the most remote places in Great Britain.

Jean has very happy memories of her time there:

"I loved Unst with all the swimming and boating. I suppose it was a bit grim in winter but you forget about that. I certainly remember swimming in Burra Firth in April – and there were no wetsuits in those days.

"There were lots of seals on the rocks there – they were beautiful grey things and the young ones were lovely – and puffins which breed there and have their nests in holes in the cliff. I spent all my time out in boats with the boys, fishing and swimming. We had a flat-bottomed dinghy which we used to rig with an elementary sail. One day Ian and the boatman's sons – the eldest was the same age as I was and the youngest the same as Ian – took me out in this sailing boat the *Juanita*. I dived over the side for a swim and after a bit I felt something coming up behind me. It was one of the seals; I had a black bathing cap on at the time so perhaps it thought I was one of them. Anyhow it gave me quite a fright although I'm sure it meant me no harm.

"I caught my first salmon there too, but I didn't know how to kill it. I had to get the boys to do it. I suppose I must have been a bit of a tomboy at that age. There was an occasion when I went to separate our cat, Pussy, who was fighting with a wild cat and it bit me. Mum called out the doctor who looked at my hand all covered in blisters and rough skin and turned to my mother and said, "Is this a boy or a girl you've got?" Mother said, "Yes, I don't know what to do with her", to which he replied, "Let her stay like that as long as you can!"

"There were masses of Shetland ponies wandering on their own over the hills; in the autumn they were rounded up and panniers put on their backs to carry peat back from the hill. They were quite tame and you could approach them. I wanted to have one to keep but Dad wouldn't allow it: I got a bicycle instead.

"I used to go to whist drives and concerts in the village hall – on my bicycle. I still have a set of spoons that I won in one of the competitions there. Dad used to play his violin and his banjo and I used to dance the sword dance and the highland fling at the concerts. The Shetlanders have strong Norse origins and many spoke in the Shetland dialect. I learned to knit there – Shetland style; we had belts made out of seal skin and one needle was held in the

Jean with Ian (right) and the boatman's son: Burrafirth, Unst

belt while you did the knitting with the other one. It was different from the usual method.

"A special event was the longest day of the year when everyone would go up onto Herma Ness at midnight to watch the sun skimming along the horizon without ever setting. It was a wonderful sight."

And it was on Unst that Jean had her first real romance: William Matheson was his name. What a different turn her life would have taken if she had married a Shetlander.

For Ian Clark also, it was one of the best times of his life. He takes up the story.

"In addition to the four keepers and their families, there was a boatman responsible for the motorboat which made fortnightly relief trips to the lighthouse and transported all the stores and fuel. These were landed annually by the lighthouse ship *Pole Star* based at Stromness, Orkney. The boat was named *Grace Darling*, and was manned by the boatman and local crofters. The boatman had two sons aged 16 and 13. One of the keepers also had a daughter a little younger than me but they moved shortly after our arrival. I became great pals with the boatman's elder son, who had a dory of his own in which we frequently went fishing, catching flat fish and sea trout on set lines. When the haddock were in, his father used a bigger boat to set lines out at the entrance to the firth. One evening we were doing this when a huge fin appeared about 30 yards from the boat. I nearly died of fright, but they told me it was merely a basking shark which does not harm people. "Another way of catching fish was to take a piece of fencing wire, about four feet long, hammer one end flat, file a barb at the other end, then walk along the shallows of the sandy beach and spear flat fish. This was quite easy and I frequently caught as many as a dozen at a time.

"Unfortunately, about 18 months after we arrived on North

Unst, the boatman died and the family moved away. However, he was replaced by his nephew, who lived with his brother; they were both in their twenties. The two brothers were very good to me and, provided I pulled an oar, they would take me out in the boat with them. During the school holidays I was on the boat every day – a wonderful training for my later life in the Navy.

"I loved the life on the island: the wildlife, the boating and fishing, and the freedom to roam. One of the keepers had a Labrador dog called Laddie: he went everywhere with me, over the hills and along the cliffs.

"My only pal was Peter, a boy who lived in a croft two miles over the hill. It was all right in the summer months when it never really got dark but in the winter the light went around 3 pm. If I was over at Peter's, like all boys I tended to delay leaving, which meant that it was dark when I came back over the hill on my own. It was very spooky at times seeing will o'the wisp on the moor or the northern lights playing along the horizon. To make matters worse the Shetland people, with their Norse background, were very superstitious: there was much talk about ghosts and the peeri folk, trolls, etc. ('peeri' is the Shetlandic word for "small"). There were numerous heaps of stones where old crofts had been and I could visualise all sorts of things. Needless to say it never taught me to leave earlier.

"The area around Unst can be very stormy and, on one occasion, waves pushed over a two-hundredweight stone on the lighthouse wall and on at least three occasions, trawlers ran ashore. A few weeks before we arrived, the trawler *May Island* had run aground against the cliffs and sank immediately. The tragedy was only discovered the following day when a crofter walking along the cliffs saw all the floating wreckage. Shortly afterwards two bodies surfaced and the motorboat went to recover them. We kept a frequent watch on the trawlers' radio waveband. If the gales were from the SE, S or SW, trawlers would come into Burrafirth to shelter. During one severe gale there were 29 trawlers there. It was almost like a small town when you saw their lights. We used to go down to exchange eggs for fish.

"In the summer months the seabird life was fantastic: gannets, kittiwakes, puffins, guillimots, razorbills by the thousand. There were also skuas, both Great Arctic and Richardson, which preyed on other birds. The greater black-backed gulls wrought havoc among the eider ducks and ducklings. Some cliffs were absolutely crammed with nesting birds but come winter they had all moved on apart from the gulls and eider ducks.

"Every day the keeper, who was ashore for a fortnight, walked two and a half miles to the top of Herma Ness, a hill opposite the lighthouse, which was about a mile off shore. At 11 a.m. he would hoist a flag to confirm that he was there; then he would pass messages by semaphore. On one occasion the message was that Dad had a perforated duodenal ulcer so the motorboat was sent to bring him ashore. It was impossible to get him to hospital but with the help of a local doctor he made a full recovery – or so it seemed at the time.

"During the summer of 1937 the *Grace Darling* went out to the lighthouse every day when the weather was suitable, with sand, gravel and cement. This was for the foundations of the wireless mast being built. It was completed in 1939 thus ending the daily walks up Herma Ness.

"Norwegian fishing boats frequently came into Baltasound at weekends and sold four fair-sized ling for a shilling. I would borrow a shilling from Mum and trudge the six miles over the hills to Baltasound, buy four ling and trudge back. It was worth it as I sold the ling for a shilling each – not a bad profit. Looking back it must have been a fair effort carrying that weight back over the rough ground and I must have been fit with all that hill walking. Being well practised in rowing, I also made a bit of pocket money by rowing in the regatta held at Baltasound.

"There were no proper shops on Unst in which to spend my money. There was a corrugated hut that sold groceries and there was a Jewish peddlar from Lerwick, who came round the islands on foot. At all stations, if anyone was going near a shop they took orders from all the houses. Clothes were obtained from JD Williams of Manchester by mail order, 'cash on delivery'. It was my dream at that time to own a pair of thigh length rubber boots and that was how I obtained mine. Mind you, in the summer we ran about in bare feet by choice.

"Sundays were rather hectic as I was sent off to Sunday School at Haroldswick in the afternoon which meant a six-mile round walk. Then in the evening Mum, Jean and I and Dad, if he was ashore, walked again to Haroldswick to church.

"There was a plentiful supply of lamb on the island. Each autumn the sheep were brought down from the hills and the lambs sold for ten shillings each. A number were bought by the keepers and put in an enclosure at the home station. Then they were killed as required – no abattoir – and shared between the families and also sent out to the lighthouse. The sheepskins were used as rugs – lovely on cold stone floors before the days of central heating. Beef was a different matter: if a crofter had a cow that he wished to kill, he went round with a little book taking orders until it was worthwhile killing the beast. Nothing was wasted.

"I attended the two-teacher school at Haroldswick, three

The Shore Station at Burrafirth, now Visitor Centre for the Herma Ness Nature Reserve

miles over the hill. Haroldswick was not really a village but more the centre of a number of crofts dotted here and there. On coming home from school one day I was told that a dead whale had floated alongside the pier by the lighthouse. The next day the motorboat was going to tow it out to sea. My father was on the lighthouse at the time so I pleaded with my mother to let me stay off school to go with it but she wouldn't agree. Imagine my disgust later when Dad said I could have gone.

"In June 1938 Jean was old enough to start nursing. She, Mum and I travelled down to Cockenzie in East Lothian. Dad was to follow some weeks later. It being term time, I went to the local primary school for a few weeks. It was during this time that the Empire Exhibition was held in Glasgow so I paid a visit and was amazed by the things there I'd never even thought about. On the way home I bought a budgerigar which I called Chalkie. Being the first such bird seen on Unst it was, needless to say, quite an attraction and all the children came to see him.

"During this period I learnt to swim. Very few lighthouse children could swim and I can recall at least three occasions when children were drowned. At most stations the water was too dangerous for learners.

"There was great community spirit on Shetland. Even though the crofts were widely spaced, in the summer with the long hours of daylight when it was never completely dark, everyone was busy on the land and at sea. But in the winter it was dark by 3 pm and this was the time for dances. About once a month a dance was held in the local corrugated iron village hall. They started at about 8 pm and finished at about four the following morning. As people had walked a long way, they made the evening last. The music was provided by fiddlers – most Shetland men could play the fiddle and the women took turns on the piano. It was mostly old-time reels, jigs, hornpipe with the occasional 'modern' dance. There was a break when vast amounts of food were consumed, followed by a 'sing-song' – then back to the dancing. At that time there were no licensed premises on Shetland so any alcohol was of the home-brewed variety. We also used to have herring 'n tatty suppers – salt herrings and potatoes. Needless to say, a dance went along with it.

"Weddings were big occasions and everyone attended. The local hall was used for the reception and close friends of the bride provided the food for the long trestle tables. The food consisted of dried lamb and vegetables followed by piles of baking.

"After the service which was held in the nearby corrugated iron church, the lady-providers set off for the hall to put the kettles on. Meanwhile the remainder, headed by the bride and groom, all arm in arm, children included, went for a walk which lasted about half an hour, ending up at the hall with a fusillade of shotguns. Everyone then set to and demolished the heaps of food. The hall was then cleared and dancing commenced. At ten o'clock the tables were then set out again for more food. Dancing recommenced until about 4 am when all those who were fit enough staggered home. So much for the first night. The second night was for relatives and close friends gathered in the hall: this time from 8 pm to about 1 am when more food and dancing was enjoyed. All was not yet over as, on the third night, the women who had provided the catering gathered in the hall for a much smaller feast.

"All good things come to an end. In my case it was passing the qualifying examination (similar to the 11+ in England) in May 1939, which meant that I would have to go into lodgings in Lerwick to attend the Grammar School. It was then decided that I should go to stay with Bessie and attend Preston Lodge, also a grammar school, at Prestonpans in East Lothian. I travelled down with Mum and Dad, never to return to my beloved Unst.

"I am sometimes asked if I feel disadvantaged by being brought up in the wilds away from civilisation. On the contrary, I loved the life with the freedom to wander wherever I wanted; in addition I served a wonderful apprenticeship in small boat handling which paid off in my later career."

6

Haddington & Marriage

IN 1938 JEAN LEFT HOME and followed her sisters Bessie and Lena to train as a nurse at Headington Mental Hospital just outside Edinburgh. She stayed there until 1944, completing her training and gaining her diploma.

Jean: "At this point, Mum and Dad decided that it was time for me to start work. Bessie was married and living in Port Seton; Lena was also nursing in Haddington and Bert was in Leith. As Ian would have been left on his own with Dad – not a good arrangement as Dad was away on the lighthouse for three weeks in four – he travelled south with us. We travelled by boat from Baltasound to Lerwick then on to Aberdeen on a ferry ship; then by train to Port Seton. The trip through the North Sea was very stormy and, strangely as I had spent so much of my time on the water, I was terribly sea-sick; when I got off the ship at Aberdeen my legs had gone and I couldn't find the ground.

"After the freedom of life on the islands I didn't like training as a nurse much, but my sister Lena made me stay. We had to wear these three-quarter length uniforms with stiff white collar and terrible thick black stockings. My first jobs were to wash the bandages, remove the ashes and reset the fire. Then the dirty sheets had to be soaked in Jeyes Fluid in the bath, before being sent to the laundry.

"Looking back, there was much that was wrong with the treatment of mental patients at that time. Many were not so seriously handicapped that they could not have stayed at home but often their families just didn't want them. The worst patients were put in side wards where it was common practice for them to start breaking the windows. Two grams of paraldehyde was the standard treatment.

Nurse Jean Clark

"There were very strict rules in the nurses' home. The nurses were allowed one late pass a week; any extra late passes had to be paid for – 2/6d, which went to the Red Cross. All the nurses had to hang their keys on the board inside the door before they went out. Miss Stevenson, the Matron, used to stand by the gate to watch the nurses returning, ready to check any keys still hanging on the board.

"On one occasion a few of us missed the last bus and had to walk from North Berwick to Haddington. Matron was waiting for us and told us to report to her the following morning at 9 am. "And what were you doing last night?"

"She was taken ill shortly after I left nursing and I went to visit her in hospital. "So, Nurse Clark, you *did* marry a Pole then," she said. Actually she rather liked them herself but her sole companion remained her Labrador dog, which she used to exercise in the grounds after the 10.30 pm curfew!

"I loved dancing and there were dances in the town hall, Haddington, at Tranent and North Berwick. Also the Palais de Dance in Edinburgh. I met Jan at a dance at the School Hall at Knox School, Haddington in 1941. He asked me to dance a tango! We arranged to go to the pictures the following day and the romance began. The following day we had arranged to meet at another dance hall. Lena and I had bought the tickets in advance but, when we got there, there was no sign of Jan and Piotr, so we sold the tickets back. Unfortunately they had already got their own tickets and were inside the hall."

The Poles were not very popular with the local youths as they provided very stiff competition for the favours of the local girls: the native boys were no match for their smart uniforms and hand-kissing customs. The courtship, like so many in the war, was an intermittent affair with Jean and Jan spending time together whenever he could get leave and she could get days off from the hospital. Jan was stationed at Gosford near Aberlady.

Jean: "When I had the day off, I would stay at Bessie's in Musselburgh. One day after a dance at Gosford, I missed the last bus at 10.20 so Jan got me a bicycle. It was of

Nurse Clark in the grounds of Haddington Hospital

course the blackout and on the way home there was a fork in the road – which I didn't notice – and I went over the handle-bars. I was wearing a kilt and skinned my knees. Bessie said that she would have stayed the night in the camp! Jan arranged for the bicycle to be collected from a garage by some of the regiment the next day."

Jean's parents were not pleased to hear of her intention to marry Jan. Her father, often one to come up with a wise observation, advised: "Troubles are not to seek; they'll come to you". And there were further complications: Jan's unit was transferred to another station, Lanark near Glasgow, and then he was sent on a course in Catterick in Yorkshire. What is more it was Advent, and they had to be given special dispensation for the marriage to be held.

In the end, they were married in St Mary's Catholic Church in Haddington on 7 December 1943. It was 2 o'clock on a Friday afternoon. The Best Man was Piotr, a Polish comrade and the bridesmaid, sister Lena. Bessie had refused to come as she disapproved of Jean converting to Catholicism. Some of Jean's nurse friends attended and four or five Poles including Jan's commanding officer, a tall man with a monocle – later killed in France on the first day of fighting. There were about fifteen people all together.

In spite of his disapproval, John Clark organised and paid for the reception: tea and drinks, which was held at the Railway Inn, run by a Mr and Mrs Russell.

Jean: "After the wedding we took a room in a house on Hawthorn Bank Road in Haddington. We both had a week's leave so we spent a few days in Fidra and some in Edinburgh including some dancing at the Palais de Dance. Then Jan was transferred to Bury St Edmunds and, three days after we were married, as I had married a foreigner, I had to register with the local police as an alien. First I stayed with my sister Bessie in Victoria Terrace, Musselburgh, but I

Jean and Jan's wedding, 1943; Jean's sister, Lena, and Best Man, Piotr

was required to notify them of any change of address – it's all recorded in my identity card which I still have."

In September 1939 Ian, who was staying with Bessie and her husband, started school at Preston Lodge – although the outbreak of war put the start of term back by a week – and Jean had started nursing at Haddington. Then in mid-1940, Bessie moved house to Musselburgh and Ian changed to Musselburgh Grammar School. But the following year, John Clark was appointed Keeper at Fidra. This was a very convenient move for Jean and Ian: Ian was now able to spend the holidays and the occasional weekend at home, while Jean was able to visit from the hospital on her days off. She would go by bus to North Berwick and then her father used to come and meet her in his boat. Meanwhile Bert, now 21 and in the Royal Army Medical Corps, was posted to Burma.

Ian: "The weather was very hot during the remainder of the summer of 1939 and most of my time was spent in Port

Seton swimming pool. Compared to Unst I found life very tame.

"However war broke out in September. One evening we were down by the harbour and we could see quite a large ship making its way up the Firth of Forth; suddenly it went up in a sheet of flame having detonated a magnetic mine and was a total loss. The ship was the *Silvestra* owned by Salveson of Leith, a whale factory ship returning from the Arctic whaling season.

"About a month later we were on the playing fields on a Wednesday afternoon when we suddenly heard the roar of aircraft engines not far overhead. A German Heinkel bomber flew over pursued by a Spitfire firing its machine guns. The German plane crashed into the Firth and a fishing boat from Port Seton picked up the crew. The war had arrived at our very doorstep."

Fidra is a small rocky island just off the coast of East Lothian near the small town of Yellowcraigs, half a mile off shore from North Berwick. RL Stevenson described the strange, grey island of two humps in *Catriona*. The island is now part of a nature reserve managed by the Royal Society for the Protection of Birds. The tower of Fidra lighthouse, engineered by David and Thomas Stevenson in 1885, is only 55 feet high but the beacon has a range of 24 nautical miles. At night there are four white light flashes every 30 seconds. It was automated in 1970.

Ian: "It was quite handy travelling by bus to Dirleton and then by foot down to the beach. A path led through the minefield where Dad met me with the rowing boat. Fidra was great – more like Unst, as far as I was concerned. There were only four people on the island: Mum, Dad, the second keeper and his wife. He had two rowing boats, one of them being light enough for me to launch by crane from the pier. I spent most of the summer holiday catching fish, some of which were used as bait for my lobster creels. Lobsters were plentiful due to wartime fishing restrictions.

"During this time my sister Bessie, who was six months pregnant, was due to visit us for a few days with her three year old daughter, Merle. On the day in question there was still the tail end of an easterly gale and there was quite a sea running into the gully where we launched the rowing boat. As Bessie had already started on her way, we had to launch the boat to pick her up. We made for the nearest beach where breakers were running to land, so that Dad could walk three-quarters of a mile through the minefield to meet Bessie. Then I had to row round a small headland into more sheltered waters where I dodged about a bit until they came back. I can tell you I was glad to make it as the sea was very rough. When Bessie and Dad arrived I took the boat back into the beach to pick them up and we set off. But once we had cleared the headland the seas were worse and it was too dangerous to land at the pier on the east side of the island so we landed on the west side, pulled the boat up onto the shingle and returned it to the pier the next day.

"Each evening two trawler minesweepers responsible for sweeping the approach channel to the Forth would anchor in the Bay of Fidra. We got to know the crew well, supplying them with lobsters and on one occasion my pal and I spent a day at sea with them while they were carrying out a practice shoot against aircraft-towed targets.

"There were no guns on Fidra but there was a battery of 6 inch coastal defence guns manned by the Royal Artillery on a nearby headland towards Gallen. When using our rowing boat we were required to notify them by telephone to avoid an accident.

"I left school in 1942 after taking my 'lowers' (equivalent to O levels) and spent the holidays on Fidra. During this time the other keeper was due to go on a fortnight's leave but no relief was available. The temporary reliefs were done by what were known as 'occasionals' – usually a local man – but being wartime, everyone was fully occupied. I was not quite 16 but Head Office in Edinburgh knew me and agreed to my becoming relief keeper. The work wasn't too hard as, during the war, the light was only lit on telephone instructions from the Naval authorities, when, for instance a convoy of British Naval ships was about. Some weeks later, I joined the lighthouse ship *May* based at Granton."

This extract from an article in the *Scottish Magazine* of May 1991 is by Margaret Peat, whose uncle, Mr Cordiner from Peterhead, was John Clark's successor as assistant lighthouse keeper on Fidra.

"Landing in the tiny harbour was usually made without difficulty. It was well sheltered from the westerlies and frequently awash with purple jelly fish. From the edge of the flat concrete track the steep hill rose sharply beyond

Jean and Jan with Jean's parents in the keeper's house at Rubha nan Gall, Tobermory

the blue chapel on the left and the 'white lady' on the right. Concrete was embedded with rails for guiding the bogey to transport heavy goods from the harbour to the store. It was man-powered, one to each handle, winding a cable with a winch just outside the main lighthouse wall – a heavy and relentless task when the coal or water supplies came from Granton on the lighthouse ships the *Pharos* or the *May*. One of these came fortnightly with mail, more durable provisions and other supplies necessary to maintain a lighthouse.

"At the top the track flattened out, turned the corner and terminated at the end of the lighthouse buildings. The tower was not high – a storey or so above the flat-roofed houses. Each was identical with a kitchen, living room, a tiny scullery, hallway, three bedrooms and a large walk-in store. There were no taps or bathrooms. Heating and cooking facilities were provided by the kitchen range and lighting by Tilly and paraffin lamps. The Elsan toilets were beyond the main building, handily situated near the cliff face where all the rubbish was jettisoned if it could not be burned. Single storey buildings adjacent to the main block comprised a workshop with forge, an oil store for paraffin tanks and a wash house with taps of running rainwater. Large tanks around the buildings collected the rainwater but similar tanks held drinking water brought in barrels from Granton. In this pre-plastic age it was essential to know the difference between the two heavy iron water containers in the scullery. Clear of the main block was another store for animal feed, paint, cement etc. and a wooden shed for wireless communication with Fifeness Coastguard. This would concern weather and any unusual sightings.

"Inside the house the rooms facing west were bright and spacious. At that time heavy furniture was provided by the NLB as well as excellent bedding, linen and some kitchen equipment. Most houses had three bedrooms, as occasional keepers, officials and supernumeraries had to be accommodated. During the war a Morrison air raid shelter – fortunately never used for its intended purpose – served as an extra bed with a mattress on top. These shelters were issued to all lighthouses during the war as a number had been machine-gunned or bombed. At Fair Isle South two lighthouse keepers and a daughter were killed by bombs.

"Even during bread rationing, we had ample supplies from Brodie's of North Berwick. The fresh meat ration came weekly by *Caithness Lass* from Eeeles in North Berwick with some groceries from Dunn's. Milk was either tinned or from the Fidra goats. The goats were not naturally wild and each had a name and a personality. The dreaded billy was the only wild one and grew so fierce he was eventually exiled to Hyskier." (This was obviously a cover story for the children. "In fact", says Ian Clark, "the goat got into the wash house and ate washing soda leading to a slow painful death. I was on leave at the time and helped to bury it.")

"Behind the walled and railed area in front of the houses was where the soft soap washing was hung – hopefully out of reach of the goats. There was also a vegetable patch and a hen house; the other vegetable patch, yard and hen house were in an enclosed walled area further down the island.

"Past the rail cliff edge beyond the summit flagpole was out of bounds but, given the right tide, scrambling over the seaweed rocks through the 'white lady' and exploring the small cave beyond was permitted. Rumour was that the cave went under the island even under the sea all the way to Dirleton castle. The castle rock or Castle Tarbet across the isthmus could easily be climbed from the grassy slopes facing Yellowcraigs. The top was flat and spacious, marvellous for sunbathing and desert dreams. Sometimes seals basked along the cliff face. At the other end again over the isthmus was a tiny sandy beach flanked by the fissured crop nearest the mainland. It was visible only at low tide but we knew when the tides came and went. After all we had to get back across the isthmus before it flooded; this was only to a foot or so – unless it was a spring tide.

"On Fidra now, the natural features remain, and a myriad of terns nest and wheel beyond the ruined wall, but almost all evidence of human occupation has gone. The outbuildings have vanished, the houses stare blindly from walled windows; an automatic light, however bright, needs little human contact."

It was while Keeper on Fidra that John Clark was diagnosed with further duodenal ulcer problems, the condition that was to lead to his death a few years later. This probably prompted the NLB to move him to a less demanding posting.

Footnote: the 'white lady' is a gap in the rock. With the sky behind, the shape resembles a woman.

7
Jan's War

JAN ZWOLIŃSKI JOINED THE POLISH Army in 1937 at the age of twenty. There are no details of his first two years in the military, doing what the British would describe as 'National Service' but presumably they were spent in basic training. Whatever form that took, it was to be put into practice all too soon. In September 1939, Nazi Germany invaded Poland from the west but there was no haven to the east where the equally aggressive Russians were also advancing. The totally inadequate and under-armed Polish forces put up a desperate show of resistance against the German forces but they never stood a chance against this double invasion. Resistance collapsed and heavy losses were incurred, the survivors being interned in Hungary. The concentration camp in which they were kept seems to have been quite a relaxed sort of place and, although the internees were disarmed, they were allowed to keep hand pistols. They were also allowed out of camp in small groups, accompanied by an armed guard. Apparently the standard method of escape was to take the guard off to some bar and ply him with drink. When he was completely intoxicated, three or four of the group would make off to a prearranged rendez-vous where some locals, sympathetic to the Poles, would put them onto a train, heading through Austria to France. Somehow, this troop movement was being orchestrated by supporters of their leader, Colonel Stanisław Maczek. It is difficult to know how the Poles managed to re-group in France – and no doubt many did not make it – but at this time there were estimated to be some 82,000 men from Poland or émigré families in France. On 4 January 1940 General Władysław Sikorski and the French Premier signed a

Jan Zwoliński in 1939

military agreement to form a Polish Army in France and to set up a Polish government-in-exile.

Like many former combatants, Jan was immensely proud

of his achievements in the war but reluctant to talk about them afterwards. Also, of course, most soldiers are preoccupied with the events around them: with carrying out orders, implementing their training and with survival; unless they are very senior officers, they are unlikely to have much awareness of the bigger picture. What we do know is that, throughout the war, Jan served under General Maczek's command, a charismatic man for whom he had the highest respect and admiration. So knowing Maczek's movements and with the help of reports, photographs and the occasional reminiscence, we can piece together quite a clear idea of where Jan was and what he did.

Despite equipment shortages, plans were put in motion to form three infantry corps: a Grenadier Division, the 2nd Rifle Division and the Independent Rifle Brigade. They also planned to form an armoured division, up to 20 air force squadrons and auxiliary services. The Grenadier Division was based at Colombey-les-Belles, southwest of Nancy in Lorraine; the 2nd Rifle Infantry Division (2DSP), commanded by Brigadier-General Bronisław Pruger-Ketling, was despatched to the front near Belfort, and the 10th Motorized Cavalry Brigade under the command of General Maczek covered the flank near Rheims. The Brigade consisted of a tank regiment and a motorized cavalry regiment, each consisting of two battalions, an artillery battery and an anti-aircraft troop – albeit equipped with seriously antiquated weapons. Photographs of Jan and his colleagues at this time show them in French uniforms.

At the end of May 1940 the French Army was near to collapse and the remnants (some 300,000 soldiers) of the British Expeditionary Force were being rescued from the beaches of Dunkirk: this was indeed "our darkest hour". The Polish Army fought on and defended their positions for as long as they could, but at best they could only delay a major assault by providing cover for retreating units which were under constant attack and bombing. Maczek threw his troops into the battle against advancing German invasion forces. They had some successes but the odds against them were overwhelming. With 500 lightly

*Map of Northern Europe showing the route of Jan's Unit,
August 1944 – May 1945*

armed men, he retreated to the unoccupied ports in the south of France and escaped to Scotland.

By this time, the French were seeking an armistice with the Germans and, on 17 June, General Sikorski arrived at the Polish Headquarters, which had moved to Bordeaux, to take stock of their position. He decided it was hopeless and appealed to Winston Churchill, who arranged for him to be flown out to the UK in an RAF plane; the Polish President and members of the government followed on the British Cruiser HMS *Arethuse*.

Immediately after the fall of France, Great Britain was on full alert under the threat of invasion. By July, a raggle-taggle collection of soldiers, the remnants of the Polish Army, many of whose campaign odysseys had taken them through Hungary or Rumania, France and North Africa, were being assembled and reorganised in Scotland, as the 1st Polish Army Corps under the command of General Marian Kukieł. Their duties were building coastal defences, initially along the coast between Fife and Angus, and being re-trained on British equipment, which was itself in desperately short supply. Within two months they had built a defensive perimeter to the north of Edinburgh, supported by the Home Guard – not then the object of ridicule it was later to become following its portrayal in the television programme, *Dad's Army*. In the lead up to what later came to be known as the Battle

Jan in Polish uniform before the war

of Britain - and the subsequent threat from Operation Sealion, the presence of almost 20,000 combat-experienced Polish troops was a significant support for the British defences.

Scotland was now the base for the Polish army: the Island of Bute became a political detention centre to screen the troops for 'fifth columnists' or those who might damage the new strategies being developed by Sikorski and the Government-in-Exile, and Inverlochy Castle near Fort William was used for the training of Special Forces known as the *Cichociemni* or the 'Silent and Unseen'.

Once the major threat of invasion was over, Britain underwent a radical transformation process in gearing up for its war effort. On 5 August, Poland signed an agreement with the British Government: this agreement enabled all Polish military forces to keep their national identity and military customs under Polish command, in conjunction with the British War Office and the British High Command. The Poles were now an integral part of the overall war strategy.

Weapon Training

Between 1940 and the spring of 1944, preparations for Operation Overlord were being made. During this period the Polish forces were managing to organise themselves into a potent force both in the air – the Polish Airborne Brigade under General Stanisław Sosabowski – and on land. On February 25 1942, the 10th Brigade was born again, this time as the 1st Polish Armoured Division (Dywizja Pancerna). It was under the command of the charismatic Maczek, now Major-General, with Colonel Kazimierz Dworak as second-in-command. The armoured vehicles were mostly tanks but Jan Zwoliński, with the rank of Sergeant, was one of the mechanical support team, travelling by armoured vehicle.

The 1st Polish Armoured Division had been training mostly in Scotland, but in May 1943 they moved to Suffolk to undergo five months of intensive training on Cromwell tanks. These exercises were carried out on the Suffolk heaths, a terrain very similar to that of northern France. They then set off for their most important and most dangerous phase of the war: Operation Overlord, the

Tank Exercises

culmination of their training over the last two years. This began with the invasion of Normandy. They landed on Juno beach on 1 August 1944, with 16,000 men and some 400 tanks. They were attached to the 1st Canadian Army and their joint role was to support the build-up of strength in the bridgehead behind the beaches, to allow the leading forces to break out and push for the strategic city of Caen.

Students of the war will be familiar with the events of the next few weeks and I shall not go into details. In essence, the plan was that the British 2nd Army under General Montgomery would take the German stronghold of Caen, forcing the Germans out into a 'pocket'. '1st Armoured' and the 1st Canadian Army would then close the end of this pocket – the Falaise gap - linking up with US forces under General Patton, near Argentan, thereby cutting off the German retreat route to the south.

The reality was rather different: the Germans put up tough resistance, and their defence of Caen, making full use of natural features, counter-attack strategies and planned withdrawals to

Jan (second from top) in Tank Training

pre-prepared positions, was textbook material for future study. Montgomery made three attempts to take the city and failed each time. This delayed the breakout by almost six weeks and it also prevented the Allies from moving into the more open countryside suitable for tanks.

The area to the south of Caen comprises two ranges of hills; in between them there is a valley through which the rivers Laizon and Dives flow into the coastal plain. The Germans not only occupied the town of Caen: they also occupied strategic positions in these hills.

The 1st Armoured Division broke camp on the night of 7 August. They worked their way up through the plain, tanks and vehicles advancing in thick clouds of dust making navigation almost impossible. They had to cross the River Laizon, which acted as an effective anti-tank ditch, and they came under heavy enemy fire; more tragically, Bomber Command, made up of Canadian Squadrons, mistook yellow flares for enemy positions and bombed their own ground forces inflicting serious casualties.

Visit of General Sikorski, King George VI and Queen Elizabeth

Jan was in the middle of this and later described it as the most terrifying experience of his life. As soon as the bombs started falling, everyone dived for whatever cover they could find. At the end of what seemed like half a lifetime, but was probably less than a minute, Jan found that he had been thrown into a ditch and covered with debris – a piece of luck that probably saved his life. He emerged to find a scene of complete carnage: bodies and body parts smouldering amongst the mangled wreckage of vehicles, the air full of dust, smoke and the stench of burning flesh. And not a flicker of life anywhere. It is not surprising that survivors had no wish to relate their experiences later.

On 15 August, Falaise was taken and the Canadian and Polish armoured vehicles were ordered to swing southeast for Trun, a town further up the River Dives, to seal the pocket. Meanwhile the Germans were fighting desperately to reach 'the gap'. Allied fighter bombers were flying over 2,000 sorties a day, inflicting massive losses, while artillery poured shells into the valley below. The Poles captured Mont Ormel ('Hill 262', a few miles east of

General Montgomery visiting the troops

Chambois); but this was a dangerous move as they had become isolated – in effect 1,500 Poles and 80 tanks were cut off from the supply lines from 19 to 22 August – but General Maczek had recognised the strategic importance of Mont Ormel and his decision to hold the escarpment and then descend into the valley to capture Chambois effectively closed the pocket. They captured 5,500 prisoners, and destroyed 70 tanks and another 500 vehicles. The destruction of the German forces at the Falaise Gap signalled the start of their withdrawal from Normandy.

On 23 August, '1st Armoured' was "put into reserve", which is 'army speak' for "given a rest". It had been a bloody three weeks and they had lost 325 soldiers, including 21 officers, and over a thousand had been wounded. They had just five days to recover, refitting and re-arming, to prepare for the next stage of Operation Overlord: the chase through northern France, which they had been rehearsing in Britain.

Northern France is flat country – perfect for tanks – but it is intersected by numerous rivers and canals. The Germans used these natural obstacles to great effect in slowing the Allies' advance. By late August the US forces were on the outskirts of Paris and had crossed the river Seine. The task of '1st Armoured', now under Canadian control, was to clear the left flank which was made up of the Channel ports. After two days of marching in mud and rain along roads unsuitable for armoured vehicles, they arrived at Elbeuf, a town just south of Rouen. On 29 August they crossed the River Seine at Elbeuf over a temporary bridge nicknamed 'Warsaw Bridge'. They then swept on northeast, liberating Amiens and pursuing the routed Germans towards Abbeville; over a nine day period they covered some 400 km, taking St. Ômer, Ypres and Roulers, capturing prisoners and equipment en route. To slow the advance, the German army stubbornly defended woodland and hills and systematically destroyed all bridges in their path.

General Maczek and '1st Armoured' crossed into Holland but his British Cromwell tanks and the light Shermans were no match for the German tanks and the Poles suffered heavy casualties.

They joined up with the British 2nd Army while the 1st Canadian Army cleared the southern part of Holland and opened the port of Antwerp. This was vital to improve the supply of frontline units since the lines of supply stretched all along the Channel Ports to Cherbourg.

The Dutch city of Breda was entered on 29 October by the 8th Polish Rifle Battalion (*8 Batalion Strzelców*). There was intense street-fighting with troops using grenades to clear cellars and dodging sniper fire in house-to-house fighting. Bunkers and well-positioned mortars, anti-tank guns and machine guns put up stiff resistance and at times the intensity of battle was ferocious. Tank support was called in for a systematic clearance district by district. There were high casualty rates to both sides but, despite local damage to property, there were, amazingly, no civilian casualties.

Jan and his colleagues were billeted with families in Breda. The Dutch had had a rough time under the Nazi occupation and they were desperately short of basic needs. The Poles, who at various times were given leave back in Scotland, were able to

The Liberation of Brussels

bring them back some food and clothing.

The liberation of Breda drew a huge outpouring of emotion from the citizens of that city: the Poles were greeted as heroes and their gratitude was to extend for as long as there were living people that remembered it. Under the disapproving eye of the Communist regime, which refused to recognise the part played by Poles on the Western front, reunions and return visits were organised, anniversaries celebrated and real friendships built. Jan and his 'veterans club' were invited to Breda for the twenty-fifth anniversary celebrations in 1968 and Jan stayed with Witold and Corry Worobiej. Witold was a Pole who had met a Dutch girl at the liberation, married her and fathered six children. He paid a second visit in 1978 and, to this day, Jean corresponds regularly with Corry and other Dutch friends in Breda, born of these celebrations.

Hitler's counter-attack had been planned in the autumn of 1944, but by mid-winter the poor weather, leaving the ground with a thick snow cover, and lack of fighter support, left the Ardennes a stagnant defensive front. For '1st Armoured', the rest

Jan (centre standing) with Polish colleagues

from frontline activity was welcomed, but the weather conditions and the billeting arrangements were far from ideal. In fact there weren't any: troops found themselves sleeping in straw-lined ditches or, the luckier ones, in farm buildings.

But they were on the move again at the beginning of April 1945 when '1st Armoured' joined the 2nd Canadian Corps for its final push towards the North Sea and the German border. It was a long and wearisome march through flooded marshes but it was here that General Maczek showed his skills, confusing the enemy with constant changes and decoys: tanks were disembarked from transporters to suggest an attack; units were moved around, some being amalgamated with others, always optimising his firepower and keeping pressure on the enemy.

By 1 May 1945 the Division was travelling north along the Dutch–German border, their target being the German naval base at Wilhelmshaven. However, before they could mount their assault on the base, on 5 May, Germany capitulated. General Maczek accepted the surrender of the base almost intact with 19,000 prisoners (including two Admirals and a General), three battle cruisers, 18 submarines, 205 minor warships and support vessels, 94 fortress guns, 159 field guns, 64 million rounds of carbine ammunition, and food for 50,000 troops. It was a happy day.

The 1st Polish Armoured Division, with the Polish Parachute Brigade, remained part of the British Army on the Rhine (BAOR) until 1947. There was no more fighting and their time was spent in security duties in Germany as the country began to return to post-war normality. Maczek was promoted to Lieutenant-General and placed in charge of all Polish forces until in 1947 they were disbanded and the troops placed in the Polish Resettlement Corps.

General Maczek was deprived of his Polish citizenship by the post-war Communist regime and stayed in Britain, but he was not recognised by the Government as a former British soldier either. Until the 1960s he worked as a barman at a hotel in Edinburgh. He died in 1994, aged 102, and is buried in the Polish military cemetery in Breda.

8
Motherhood & Mull

IN 1943, JOHN CLARK WAS moved to Rubha nan Gall lighthouse, a 'one-keeper station' near Tobermory, Isle of Mull. Jean continued nursing at Haddington until she was pregnant for the first time, when she went back to the family in Tobermory. During this time Jan was fighting in France and Holland, only occasionally returning to Britain. For a short spell he was stationed at Scarborough, but Jean's father thought it would be unsafe for her to make the journey on her own.

The lighthouse at Rubha nan Gall meaning 'Point of the Stranger' was built in 1857. It is one of the few lighthouses easily accessible from the nearest 'civilization'. A hillside path leads to the keeper's house from which the lighthouse itself is only a few yards along a causeway. Today the path to the lighthouse is a 40-minute scramble through muddy pools and over fallen trees, but according to Shuggy McAllister, who grew up there, in the 1940s it was more crowded than Main Street. He and his young friends, with nothing much to do in the school holidays, would walk along this path to the Brown Monument and on to Bloody Bay or up Jacob's Ladder to the golf course. They often used to call in on the keeper's house where they could rely on Mrs Clark for a "piece": a scone with jam and a glass of milk. The nearest neighbours were goats, some of which seemed to resent the human incursions on their territory and responded by eating the flowers in the garden and mounting guard over the path. On one occasion they stopped Bessie getting through altogether and she had to return to Tobermory until the road was clear.

Jean with Sherry at the Western Isles Hotel, Tobermory

Jean: "I was three months pregnant when I went to Tobermory, where Dad had been posted in 1943. This was in a wonderful position beside the bay and we had a lovely house there just a hundred yards from the lighthouse. We were quite self-sufficient: Dad used to shoot rabbits and there was a gamekeeper who used to snare them with traps.

"We had four goats – Snowy and Jenny were two – and Sherry, a Red Setter. The goats used to follow us to town. Dad would sometimes get a phone call from the Western Isles Hotel: "Mr Clark, come and fetch your goats; they are eating the roses". Dad milked the goats and Mum used to make cream cheese from the goats' milk. We had a vegetable garden which provided for most of our needs. Dad caught fish at the rocks by the lighthouse - Jan also when he was there. When trawlers came into Tobermory, Dad would buy cod directly from the ship."

The two babies were born at the keeper's house, Wanda in October

John Clark at the keeper's house, Rubha nan Gall, 1947

1944 and Krysia in December 1945. They were delivered by Dr McIntyre and the midwife Nurse MacMillan (one of the first MacMillan Nurses?!) who came from Tobermory on foot.

There was a further complication to life for the Clark family at this time. Their daughter Lena, then unmarried, had given birth to a baby girl, June. In those days of moral rectitude, this was an embarrassment. Lena was unable to look after the child herself in the nurses' home in Haddington and so her mother and father took over responsibility for June in Tobermory. Here the information trail goes cool, if not exactly cold. Jean to her great credit has kept in touch with June to this day – necessarily by post – but the relationship between June and the rest of the family has always been an uneasy one.

The Clarks were very popular in Tobermory. John Clark, in spite of his failing health, delighted in the proximity of a local community and threw himself into every sort of social activity. He ran a girls' dancing troupe with Bobby McLeod; Bobby McLeod, whose music later became very well known, had an accordion band that played in the Mish Nish Hotel.

Jean: "Dad taught Scottish dancing – the highland fling and the sword dance, and also some Irish dances. It was mostly in the Church Hall beside the Post Office or at the Western Isles Hotel. He would not allow me to join the troupe, although I did learn to perform the sword dance - but I could never get the hang of Irish dancing.

"My time was well taken up with two children, knitting, ripping down old jumpers, etc. We didn't have a lot of friends in the town: just the McIntyres and Daisy in the drapery shop but Bessie and Lena and other members of the family visited quite a lot, as it was a lovely place to stay. I used to visit Mrs McIntyre quite often. How I ever managed to push two children up that hill I shall never know…"

Ailsa Craig, Firth of Clyde, Ayrshire Photographs by permission of Maybole Community Council

Kirkabister Ness, Bressay, Shetland

Buchan Ness, Boddam, Aberdeenshire

Barns Ness, Dunbar, East Lothian

Rhinns of Islay, Orsay, Islay

Muckle Flugga, Unst, Shetland, the most northerly point of the British Isles. Photograph by Philip Plisson

Fidra, Firth of Forth, East Lothian

Rubha nan Gall, Tobermory, Isle of Mull

When Wanda was born, John Clark alerted the Roman Catholic priest in Oban. A search was then put under way for a suitable (i.e. Catholic) sponsor or godmother, they being, it would seem, rather thin on the ground in Mull at the time. Eventually a maid, fit for purpose, was found at the Western Isles Hotel. The priest then came over on the ferry to perform the necessary duties in the keeper's house. When it came to Krysia's baptism two years later Jan was back and the priest was a bit more canny; he brought his own sponsor from Oban, Ann Mary Beale.

Life was predominantly domestic in these months at Rubha nan Gall. With two babies to look after, Jean's hands were full although she did have her mother's help. Conditions were certainly not luxurious – were they ever at lighthouse stations? – but they had enough for their daily needs and on the west coast of Scotland at least they were comparatively safe. It was a small community and amusements were mostly home-grown: music

Jean with Sherry at the Rubha nan Gall lighthouse

and dancing of the traditional variety. Tobermory was the Head Quarters of HMS Western Isles where corvettes and frigates, on being commissioned, were sent for training as escort vessels. Apart from that, the only indications of danger were the light anti-aircraft guns fitted to the McBrain ferry from Oban: war must have seemed far away. Imagine the excitement when one day the Polish warship *Błyskawica* came to anchor in Tobermory Bay. Jan was on leave and he and John went onto the ship and took full advantage of the Polish hospitality – much to mother's disapproval!

By this time Jan had moved to Scarborough for training; then they went off to fight, first in France, then Holland; he was in Breda when Wanda was born and in Germany when Krysia was born. This was a worrying time for the whole family. There was no telephone so they kept in touch by letter, Jean writing to P27, the Polish Forces mail box, and although there were no newspapers, they listened to the news on the radio. By the time the war was over, Jan was still in Germany and he wanted Jean to go over there, but her father decided that this was unwise.

When Jan finally returned to the UK in 1947 he and the other Polish military were placed in a 'resettlement division'; this was more of a holding operation while they decided their future. The situation was a difficult one for the British authorities: they were grateful to the Poles for their wonderful support during the war but charity began at home. They had huge numbers of demobilised servicemen returning to civilian life, many of them having joined up straight from school with no qualifications, and there were very few jobs. Jan was one of those for whom employment prospects in the UK were bleak: the coal mines or the land. He was not attracted by either. Some of his friends went to Belgium then on to Canada where they did very well. Australia was another possibility as were various countries in South America although they posed language problems.

The other possibility was to return to Warsaw. There were some arguments in favour: Jan had not seen his family for eight years. His mother, of course, wanted him to return: his father had died of cancer in 1944; his younger brother Heniek had been taken to Buchenwald. Romek, Jan's elder brother, was also keen for Jan to come back but he may well have had an ulterior motive, as will be explained later. Jadzia, Jan's sister, advised against return in coded messages in her letters (as mail was likely to be censored). Jan wanted to go to South America or Belgium for reasons that are not entirely clear but John Clark was strongly against this, advising that it was madness to go to a foreign country with two small children, knowing no one and unable to speak the language. In the end, pressure from Romek, together with the offer of living

Jean with Wanda, Krysia and Sherry, Tobermory, 1946

accommodation, won the day. Jan and Jean decided to return to Warsaw.

Jean with Wanda, Krysia and Sherry, Isle of Mull, 1946

Footnote: The Mish Nish Hotel is now owned by Bobby McLeod's son and the room in which Bobby Senior played has many commemorative photographs and a sleeve of one of his LPs displayed behind the bar. His music is still available on CD.

The lighthouse at Rubha nan Gall was automated and the last lighthouse keeper left in 1960.

9
Return to Poland

THE JOURNEY BEGAN AUSPICIOUSLY WITH a week at a transfer camp at Prestwick. There they met other families that had taken the same decision: friendships were struck up with Jean McLoughlin Dąbrowska and Betty Denham Romatowska, whom Jean was to get in touch with in Warsaw. The departure was marked by the Polish band striking up a traditional Scottish farewell song:

> *For we're no' awa' tae bide awa',*
> *For we're no' awa tae le'e ye,*
> *For we're no' awa' tae bide awa',*
> *We'll aye come back an' see ye.*

The ship, the *Empress of Britain,* sailed from Leith; it was a beautiful crossing, the sea being calm as a mill pond. Less beautiful was the greeting at Gdynia where the welcoming party was a menacing semi-circle of soldiers, armed to the teeth, weapons at the ready.

Jean: "When we got to the gangway, Jan was ahead carrying the kitbag and they held me back because they had to check all my papers. I was carrying Krysia and holding Wanda by the hand. One of the crew said to me, "You'd better make your mind up: once you set foot on Polish soil, you're finished. If you want to go back we'll take you." They gave us some blankets and some 'dog biscuits' and we were away. We were loaded up onto cattle trucks. Jean Dąbrowska was with us with Stasio in his pram but Krysia had no pram so I had to sit on the luggage with her on my lap. We were taken to this camp behind barbed wire and they gave us a meal: it was ersatz coffee and brown bread. They put us in these camp beds and when they woke us up in the morning, the army was going round checking to see if we had any newspapers or other 'subversive material' – only a hint of what was to come.

"Jan's brother and his nephew, Jurek, came down to meet us. They took us out for lunch and we were in this restaurant and Jan ordered strawberry soup; we all had strawberry soup and I thought, "What sort of food do they eat in this country?"

"Then we were driven to the train and the back of the lorry flew open and all the biscuits fell out. Two or three times we were taken out, as the train was waiting – and then it wasn't waiting. Eventually we were loaded into this cattle truck and set off at ten o'clock in the evening. At three o'clock in the morning – it was daylight, of course – we could see women working in the fields. There was a band going up and down the train and they played *Warszawa moja Warszawa* – I suppose they were trying to keep our spirits up. Of course I couldn't understand a word but the melody sticks in my memory – I love that song.

"Arriving in Warsaw, we got off the train and they told us to sit on our luggage and not to move. Then they arrived with a lorry and loaded us all up. As we drove through Warsaw, the scene of destruction was unbelievable: bombed buildings and rubble everywhere. Then we arrived at Grochów, a suburb of the city on the eastern side of the River Wisła, which was Jan's family's home. We stopped at Kawcza, number 45 on the first floor and Jan met his mother whom he hadn't seen for eight years. It was an emotional moment from a woman I was soon to discover had little warmth.

"There was a meal set out on the table with vodka; I was

sitting between Jan and his mother on the sofa and they were talk, talk, talking – and I didn't understand a word! Then Jan brought in two live chickens and put them in my lap. I said, "What do you expect me to do to those?" and he said, "Kill them" and laughed. I couldn't do that – my father had always killed the chickens at home. Anyhow, they killed them and they brought me the dead birds and some vegetables: carrots, celery and onions. They wanted me to make *rosół*, a sort of chicken broth. I had arrived in Poland."

The Zwoliński family consisted of Jan's mother, Stanisława, his elder brother Romek and his sister Jadzia. Jan's father had died of cancer in 1944 and his younger brother Heniek had died at Buchenwald concentration camp. No one knows quite what happened to Heniek, but a survivor said that he had seen his dead body at the camp.

Irka Olejniczak was a near neighbour (then living at 47 Kawcza, the flat now occupied by Jean), and a friend of the family. Her father had been taken to Buchenwald together with Heniek. Irka was married but the couple had no children; they separated and later divorced. Later still, Romek married Irka, who was of course much younger than him. They bought a house in Wilanów and moved out of 45 Kawcza. Again there were no children.

Irka's mother seems to have been a dangerous, sexual predator. She is described as "a little, old woman and very unattractive" but she must have had some attractions as both Romek and Heniek had affairs with her. She said to Jean on one occasion, "I've had all the Zwolińskis except Jan," with a certain menace in her voice suggesting there was unfinished business. Heniek was about 18 or 19 at the time; she is supposed to have been expecting his child at one point.

Somehow Romek had managed to avoid the war; he had pretended there was something wrong with his leg and apparently everyone believed him. He ran a grocery and general stores shop under the flat at 45 Kawcza, which sold vodka too. He had managed to keep this and to keep out of trouble during the occupation; of course, the Germans needed people to run shops. His mother and Irka used to help in the shop.

Romek was adept at organising a comfortable life for himself. His mother doted on him. He had had a much better education than Jan and had gone on to university whereas Jan went straight into the army. Mother worked in the shop all the time and Romek travelled about doing business. Later when the shop finished, he worked in an office: by Polish standards at the time, he was comfortably off.

Number 45 Kawcza was a two-roomed flat: Romek stayed with his mother in one room and Jan, Jean and the children lived in the other. At the beginning of the war, Romek had bought a house in Wilanów, but twice the Germans had burned it down. Now he was rebuilding it and in the early days Jan would go there every day to help his brother work on it – although he was paid very little for doing so. When it was ready, Romek and his mother moved in. It should have followed that Jan, Jean and the girls took

Jean with Wanda and Krysia at Prestwick Camp before leaving for Poland

over the flat at 45. However, on the pretext that it would not be right for Jean to have to carry Krysia, who at that time had a leg in plaster, up a flight of stairs, the family moved across to a smaller ground floor flat (which Jean now occupies) at 47 Kawcza. In fact Romek had done some financial deal to his advantage. Jan knew that this was not right but, as so often before, he showed undue deference to his elder brother and gave in.

Jean and the children found Jan's mother a strange person, who showed them little affection. She was a very hard worker but she was mean. She used to take flowers from the garden of her home in Wilanów into Warsaw to sell them – just to make money. There was no need for this, as Romek was comfortably off. She was 83 when she was knocked down by a bus in the city and killed.

Jean: "I never quarrelled with her: she was Jan's mother and I had to accept her. She wasn't nasty to me and she was good to the children. But she once said to me, "Since you came into the family we've had nothing but trouble.""

That seemed an odd thing to say and it is difficult to think what she was referring to. In fact the evidence suggests that the opposite was the case. Jan, Jean and the girls were quite frequent visitors to the house in Wilanów. Romek would usually have a pleasant lunch with a few glasses of vodka and a cigar. Then he would play the piano for a while or take a nap. It was while he was sleeping one day that a beautiful potted palm they had in the house fell over and the pot broke. Jean, who was on hand, went into the kitchen for a broom, but she tripped on the way and knocked a kettle off the stove. She was badly scalded. Mother came in to investigate but, being unable to communicate in Polish at the time, Jean could not make her understand that she needed a doctor. After a while mother went off, but not to get a doctor – she came back with a new pot for the plant! And when Jan returned to the house, she told him nothing of the problem and merely sat him down for a meal.

Life was grim in these early days after the return to Warsaw. These were the worst times: it was the Stalinist period when Poland was under the leadership of Bolesław Bierut (1944 -1956). Living conditions were atrocious: whole families were crammed into one room, very often without running water and nearly always without gas or electricity. No one had any money, there was no food in the shops – and huge queues whenever any did appear; there were certainly no luxuries: no tea or coffee - Jean and her friends used to grind up acorns for 'coffee'. Dripping was a substitute for butter and strips of *słonina* for lard; dripping was turned into *szmalec*, *skwarki* (pork crackling). There were no clothes to buy: Jadzia was excellent at making up clothes from odd bits and pieces and once made a dressing gown out of an army blanket. The ingenious ways in which everything was used was remarkable. There were no banks and Jean used to keep her money in a tin box. And on top of all this there were appalling restrictions on people's freedoms and underneath the undermining whiff of the UB, *Urząd Bezpieczeństwa* (Bureau of Security). It is not surprising that some were prepared to compromise their principles by conceding to their demands for information.

Another problem was that Jan had not been trained for anything – except fighting – although with his army experience on tanks, he had become quite a skilled mechanic. Later in 1947, he found a job as a mechanic with PKS, a long distance bus company, but when they sold their mother's house in Modlyń the following year, Romek and Jan bought an Opel Olympia. Nobody in Warsaw had a car in those days, so this was something of a coup and a useful source of income. Jan maintained and repaired the vehicle, and he and his old army friend, Lucjan, drove it as a taxi; needless to say, Romek shared the takings.

10

Post-war Warsaw: the worst times

POLAND HAD NO TIME TO recover from the ravages of the Nazis from the west and the no less brutal incursions of the Russians from the east, before they were enveloped in a different sort of tyranny: Stalin's Soviet domination. Stalinism penetrated every aspect of life in post-war Poland. Statues of Stalin appeared in public places. The republic's leading industrial centre, Katowice, was renamed Stalinogród. Unsolicited gifts such as the Palace of Culture in Warsaw (known to Poles as 'Joe's Wedding Cake') and the oil pipeline, 'the Pipeline of Friendship' appeared. The Soviet way of life was upheld as the universal paragon of virtue. An attempt was even made to modify the Polish language by introducing the Russian practice of speaking in the second person plural, *Wy* (you) in place of the 'decadent' Polish custom of using the third person singular, *Pan* (Sir) or *Pani* (Madam).

The historian, Norman Davies wrote: "The ordinary citizens of a communist state were so enmeshed by petty rules and regulations, that meekness and subservience towards the authorities was the only way to ensure a quiet life. Permits, licences, and official stamps were required for most of the operations of everyday living. Passbooks, identity cards, and written permissions proliferated.... Passports for foreign travel were not issued by right, but only for approved purposes. The individual was forced to limit his habits and aspirations to the narrow parameters laid down by the ruling Establishment . . . Nonconformity of any sort was promptly punished. The militiaman and the petty bureaucrat walked tall."

Jean's daughter, Krysia, remembers these early days:

"There was a strong sense of community amongst people that lived in the same block of flats or in the same street. Mama was well known in the neighbourhood and clearly identifiable by the way she spoke Polish with a strong Scottish accent. She was well known as 'Angielka' – the English woman – the finer distinction between Scottish and English being lost on the Poles. She was a sociable person and would always greet neighbours and talk to them. Everybody knew her at the nearby market where she used to go regularly.

"Mama was busy looking after us children, particularly trying to find food supplies and thinking of different ways of preparing the limited range of food available, especially in winter. She had two particular friends that we would see almost every day: Betty Skwarek and her two children, Krysia and Stasio, and Hela with her daughter, Hania. This was company for Mama but also for Wanda and me. There were other children living nearby: Joasia from the next flat, Leszek from upstairs, Stefan from the flat in the basement, the twins Hania and Zbyszek and also Bogdan from the house two blocks away at number 45 where we had lived before. Mama did not need to think of ways of amusing us as we entertained ourselves.

"There were few toys available as there were no toy shops and no spare money anyhow, so we had to amuse ourselves in other ways. In the summer, we would play outside the moment we came back from school. There was, of course, homework to do, but there was also plenty of time for play. Hopscotch and skipping ropes were very popular and provided hours of amusement. We would pick daisies and make them into wreaths to put on our heads. There were games with pieces of string tied into different patterns round our fingers, small stones which had to be picked up while holding others in the palm of your hand; this required dexterity which developed with practice.

"During the hot summers, the favourite activity was the trip to the river Wisła. It was about an hour's walk across the fields so it was something of an expedition. All the food and drinks for the children had to be carried there and back so Mama, Betty and Hela came back exhausted at the end of the day. But we children loved it.

"The neighbours living in the same block of flats, first at Kawcza number 45, then at number 47, provided a vital network of support for Mama. As life revolved around the day-to-day business of survival, neighbours were important for social chat and moral support. The bench in the yard at the back of the house was a daily meeting place. The pace of life was relaxed so a lot of time was spent talking, exchanging news, information about what was in the shops, where to find a good piece of meat, what price the tomatoes were, which stall to get the best *kiszona kapusta* (marinated cabbage) or *biały serek* (curd cheese) or *śmietana* (soured cream). Every head of cauliflower or punnet of strawberries was carefully inspected before purchase. Getting good quality food at low prices was important. The Poles love food so you needed to spend time choosing and cooking it; it was always a central topic of conversation.

"As time went by, Mama learnt Polish, learnt to cook traditional food and became thoroughly versed in all aspects of the culture. Apart from the exchange of letters with her family and daily meetings with Betty, she had no contact with British culture for many years, and there was no access to newspapers or books in English. All news programmes on the radio from the West were jammed, although the family would cluster around the set listening to Radio Free Europe at a time of crisis, such as the invasion of Hungary and Czechoslovakia. News was strictly censored and the newspapers offered only official party versions of events.

"When the political restrictions were relaxed later on, any newspaper, book or record brought from the UK would be cherished, read or listened to many times and would occupy pride of place in the house. Mama still has LPs of Ian

McKellar, the Corries, Jimmy Shand and Jim Reeves from that period. Kocjan sent a record of Bill Haley and the Comets which was a great success.

"Visiting friends and relatives, particularly on their 'name days', was obligatory but also popular. A 'nameday' is the day of the saint of that name, so everyone knows when anyone else's 'nameday' is. My father, Jan's, nameday was on 24th June, Wanda's on 23rd June and mine on 13th March. As Mama was not brought up in this tradition, it was decided that her name should be translated as Janina. My father and mother therefore celebrated their name day on the same day, so it was a double event.

"Even in these hard times, people somehow managed to save up food to mark these special occasions. Mama had learnt to cook all the Polish dishes: there would be *śledzie marynowane* (marinated herrings), *śledzie w oliwie* (herrings in oil), various types of meats and sausage such as *boczek, szynka, polędwica, kiełbasa,* delicious tomato salad and *mizerja* (cucumber with soured cream). She would bake everybody's favourite cakes: *makowiec* (poppy seed cake), *sernik* (cheese cake), *szarlotka* (apple pie) or *napoleonka*

Warsaw in 1945

94

(custard filling in pastry and sprinkled with powdered sugar). The food was toasted with generous quantities of *wódka*. There was always a great variety of drinks; *wódka*, though, was essential: *wyborowa, żóbrowka, pieprzówka, śliwowica.* This was usually followed by brandy.

"My Uncle Romek and his sister Jadzia and her family would always be invited. There was also father's distant cousin Kazia and her son Bartek. Betty and Stasio Skwarek would also be included and so would Hela and Stefan Boryń. The children would, of course, also come. Lucjan, Jan's friend from the army, and his wife Zosia were frequent guests. There could be about fifteen adults and children. As the flat was very small, it was quite a task trying to find enough chairs to sit on and to squeeze everybody in. The party involved sitting down at the table; it was pretty squashed but the lack of space did not seem to matter. Although some food was rationed for many years, the namedays were always turned into something of a feast.

"There is no better way to appreciate very ordinary things than to be deprived of them. The Poles learnt the value of things in these post-war years. Everything was kept and nothing was wasted. New clothes were made out of old ones, sent in parcels by the family in Scotland, shoes were re-soled many times until they fell apart; my father repaired anything that was broken and once even attempted to make a coffee table out of old bits of wood. Practicality and ingenuity were essential for survival.

"My mother enjoyed Polish friendliness, their hospitality and the great feeling of camaraderie that existed amongst the people. In difficult times or moments of crisis, you could always rely on friends to go out of their way to help. You needed to know somebody who might know somebody who would get matters fixed. Friends were a lifeline to get through the bureaucratic system of controls, regulations, obstruction and officialdom – a Kafkaesque world of ministries and offices which required stamps, papers in triplicate and signatures at every turn. This was particularly important after my car accident when Mama needed to get through to the best doctor, find a place in the sanatorium or have a calliper made."

One day while living at 45 Kawcza, Krysia, who was three at the time, and Wanda were playing in the street with other children from the area. Jan and Lucjan came out of the house and got into the car that they used to drive as a taxi, which was standing outside. One of the local boys told Krysia to hold onto the bumper which she did. Lucjan, the driver, started up the car, dragging Krysia along the road. People were shouting to him to stop and eventually he realised something was wrong.

The effects of the accident were bruising and infection. They took the fluid off the knee but then it got worse again. There were no medicines available at that time and the doctor wanted to put leeches on Krysia's leg to suck out the blood. Jean thinks that if they had done that, it could have helped as the swelling was only blood from the bruising. That was when the network came to the rescue: a friend, Zosia Filipek, got her into hospital. It was impossible to do things like that without help. The doctor in charge of the case, Professor Gruca said it was tuberculosis. Jean is sure that was not TB as it would not have cleared up as it eventually did. She wanted to send Krysia back to the UK. Indeed John Clark had asked for her to be sent home, but the Polish Government said there was no necessity for that: they had all the treatment in Poland. What they did not say was that, as Jan ran a private taxi business, they would have to pay for the treatment. After discharge from hospital Krysia was taken to a sanatorium in Konstancin (at 1000 złts a day). An antibiotic would have cleared up the infection overnight – but none was available. John Clark said he could send penicillin from Britain but he would have to have an export licence; by the time it arrived it would no longer be needed or it would be too late.

Jean: "The doctor said we could expect at best a permanently stiff knee, at worst amputation; it was a poor outlook, it really was. In the end the hospital agreed to prescribe streptomycin, but still Krysia was there for three months. They gave her some lessons there as she was missing so much school. When she came home, I couldn't work as I had to stay at home to carry her around in a plaster. Outside, she had to be pushed around in a go-chair. She was told not to walk but at that age children don't really understand what is good for them and she kept walking.

"When Krysia came out of plaster, the leg had shrunk and was shorter than the other one, so they had to stretch it – a very painful process. And she had to bathe the leg in salt water every day – but we had no bath, so Pani Stefańska lent us a funnel which had been used for distilling illegal alcohol, which seemed to fit the purpose. Krysia would sit on the kitchen table for half an hour each evening with her leg immersed in the water and Pani Kwiatkowska, a particularly kind neighbour, would sit with her and talk to her. Then she had to have a calliper made with a special boot. Jan's cousin's husband was a shoemaker and he made the boots. When Krysia was seven she was still walking in a calliper. We had no money. We had to sell most of what we had in order to pay for all this. It was at this time that Jan went to work for the town taxis to help to pay the fees.

"We used to go to the sanatorium at Konstancin by train; it was about 20 kms. It was a wee train – narrow gauge. It went from Wilanów so Wanda, Jan and I used to go and see Krysia on a Saturday or Sunday. The first time, when we got to the station on the way back, there was a train standing there so I took Wanda and we got on it. Unfortunately the train, instead of going to Warsaw, was going the other way. It went very slowly so I could have jumped off, but I didn't want to risk it with Wanda so I waited until the next station. I had no money and so I walked back along the railway line. Jan was most unsympathetic: "You've got to look where the train is going. You might have ended up in Paris."

When Krysia was better and went back to hospital, the doctors could not believe her recovery and she was the centre of attention. But it had been a bad episode – a misfortune developing into a crisis due to the conditions at the time.

Some of the immigrants were even worse off than the Zwoliński family in post-war Poland. Jean had met Betty Denham Romatowska in Haddington through Lena, who had introduced them. She and her husband Teddy had come to Poland on the same ship from Leith, when they were expecting their first child. They went to live in Toruń. Teddy worked in the '*administracja*' – just one of those dozens of occupations in a communist state where they were paid very little and did even less. Sometime later Betty sent Jean a letter saying that she was coming to Warsaw with her children.

Jean: "It was Jadzia's nameday and we were all going over to visit her. By 2 o'clock Betty hadn't arrived and so we went off to Jadzia's without her. When we came back at 9 o'clock at night, there was Betty and the three children sitting on the stairs; they had been round to Betty Skwarek's but no one

Christmas in Warsaw. Left to right: Jean Dąbrowska, Jadzia, Krysia, Wanda, Jan, Babcia Zwolińska, Edek Rogulski

knew where I was. And these children, they were filthy; they were all out in spots and scratching themselves. They were lacking vitamins and proper food. This was at the end of 1947 and we were living in just the one room, so they all had to sleep on the floor.

"I went to visit them in Toruń once. I found them in a dreadful state: they had no food and no money. I didn't have any money either, so I sold my watch and told them to go out and buy some food. And I told Betty, "Don't have any more children. How are you going to look after them?" And she said "Oh, the church is against that sort of thing." She was a Catholic convert too.

"One day – it was about this time as Krysia still had her leg in plaster of Paris – Betty Romatowska knocked on the door with an American friend. She said that she was desperate to get back to Britain and wanted me to take her to the British Embassy, so Jan took us in the car. The Consul was very nice but said there was nothing she could do about it: Betty could only get a passport from the Polish Government. She also told us that when we went out of the building the police would stop us. She said, "Just act normally."

"We walked out into Aleja Róż and a policeman came out of his box on the other side of the road. (All the foreign embassies were under constant surveillance during this period from police boxes opposite the entrance.) He asked for my ID card but I didn't have one because I had lost it. So they took us to the police station in Piękna. It was a dreadful scene, mostly made up of serious drunks. They told me to empty my bag and asked me what I was doing in the Embassy. I explained that Betty had come from Toruń and, as she didn't know Warsaw, I thought it would be nice to help her. He said, "Well if you want to go there go yourself, don't take anyone with you because that's the way to get yourself into trouble." I was there over two hours and they had reduced me to tears. I said, "You're a policeman. I've got a brother who is a policeman and in Britain policemen try to help people; you just try to scare them to death. Nobody knows where I am and I've got a child in plaster of Paris at home...." I don't think anyone had spoken to him like that before.

"Later Betty went back to Britain with her four children. She went to Social Services in Haddington and they looked after her until her husband came over. But they had to wait for two years before he got a passport. Teddy was very clever with his hands; he used to mend watches and do shoe repairs so they were able to earn a living. I believe the children did very well when they grew up."

In these grim times, any contact with home, any reminder of happier days, any sound of an English – or better still a Scottish – voice, any glimpse of a British face was a sheer joy. Imagine then Jean's surprise when standing in the queue at the Housing Department in ulica Karowa, one day, when the young woman in front of her pulled out a handkerchief with "Bonny Scotland" written across it. This was Alice Fronckiewicz and the beginning of a friendship that lasted for years. It turned out that Alice's

Jean with Wanda, Krysia (leg in plaster) and the Opel involved in the accident

husband, Jurek, had fought in the same Polish Army Division as Jan – although they did not know each other in the war. Jurek belonged to the General Maczek Club in Warsaw and he and Jan were to meet regularly over the next fifty years: it was Jurek that arranged the military aspects of Jan's funeral in 1998.

Jean McLoughlin Dąbrowska, with Heniek her husband and their six-month-old boy, had travelled on the ship with Jan and Jean from Leith. In the confusion of the arrival in Warsaw, the two families had gone off to get transport for their baggage and had waved each other goodbye. They each knew the streets in which the other was living – but not the numbers. Jean walked the length of ulica Jagielońska – a very long road – in vain, but ulica Kawcza is much shorter and enquiries at one of the local shops for Angielka led Jean Dąbrowska to Jean's doorstep. It was to become a friendship vital to both of them. Sadly, two or three years later, she decided that she could not bear life in Poland, left Heniek, and returned to Falkirk on her own with her son, Stasio.

However hard life was in post-war Warsaw, there were some times of relief. Jan had a cousin Zosia Skotnicka, the daughter of Babcia Zwolińska's sister, also called Zosia, who had married a vet, Bolek Polubiec. They were living in Lublin but when the population relocation started after the war, moving Poles from the East to German occupied territories in the West, the family moved to Trzebiatów near Kołobrzeg. This was an agricultural region but also near the sea. The Polubiec family lived in a beautiful house which Jean remembers as "enormous but dark, with lovely antique furniture and full of plants"; there was also a big garden. For several years in the 1950s Jean and Jan and the children were guests at Trzebiatów for 'bucket and spade' holidays. Bolek Polubiec's veterinary work took him around all the farms in the area: one good turn frequently deserved another and he would return from his rounds with farmers' produce – an absolute godsend in those times of food shortage. So these were days of sunshine, sea and sand and plenty on the table - happy memories indeed.

Bolek and Zosia had two sons, Janusz, born in 1952, and Andrzej, three years younger; they were babies in those years, but the younger son Andrzej developed a very close relationship with Jean and Jan that he has maintained to this day. Although for some years he has lived and worked in Sweden, Andrzej has been a frequent visitor to Warsaw, often came with Jan and Jean on their visits to Britain and Holland and, since Jan's death, has had Jean to stay with him in Sweden. He has been a wonderful and loyal friend.

In 1951, Jean's adored father John Clark died. It was quite unexpected and the shock and grief was compounded by the unwillingness of the Polish Government to issue a passport to enable Jean to attend the funeral.

"After Dad had retired from the lighthouse service, he and Mum lived in a flat in Tobermory. He wanted to come out to Poland to see how I was. He couldn't afford the cost of a flight but thought that, with his naval skills, he could work his passage. Sadly he died before he could arrange it: he had a haemorrhage and by the time the lifeboat had got him to Oban

At Romek's house, 1952. Left to Right: Krysia, Jean, Romek, Babcia Zwolińska, Wanda, Renia (Jurek's wife), Jurek (Jan's cousin), Jadzia's son

and they operated, it was too late. Ian wrote and told me that Dad had died. I was dreadfully upset."

John Clark was buried in Oban Cemetery on 24 December 1951. It was not until four years later, in 1955, that restrictions were slightly eased and Jean and the children managed to make their first return visit to Britain.

"We flew to Belgium and then to Heathrow. I went with the two children and Betty came with her two. The husbands had to stay behind as 'deposit'. We stayed for three months, first in Chelmsford with Ian and Mary; then with Bessie in Victoria Terrace, Musselburgh. On arrival the children had no clothes. Mum and Bessie fitted them out: Clark's shoes, identical dresses, coats and berets; their plaits were cut off and they were completely transformed. Even medical needs were attended to: Krysia had sinus trouble and her tonsils were removed in Edinburgh.

"Lena was still working at Haddington Hospital so I went back there to do some night duty to earn some money. Mum looked after the children. After that, we went to see Bert. Bert had returned from Burma after the war. He then took a job in Hull with a successful fish merchant and married Renie, the boss's daughter – or the other way round. We were not sure about the order of these two events. Anyhow, Bert and Renie had a lovely house in Beverley, near Hull and two children about the same age as Wanda and Krysia. We were bowled over by the luxury in which they lived. For the children it was amazing: when they opened the cupboard, toys fell out!"

11
Hela and Betty's Stories

J EAN HAS HAD A VERY special friendship with three women that lasted for over fifty years. They come from quite different backgrounds: Betty McNichol was a Scot, Hela Żywiczyńska was a Pole and Ada Matthews was Welsh. They, like Jean, all married Poles and returned to stricken Warsaw after the war. All had children of similar ages to Jean's and hardly a week has passed since those days when they have not spent time together. Sadly Ada died in 1984, but I am grateful to her sister Gwen and her niece Jennifer for a brief account of her background.

It was at one of Lady Bertroud's parties for British born wives in the British Embassy that Jean met Ada. Ada was from Tontyberen, a small village near Caernarvon in Wales. She had an elder brother Mervyn and a younger sister, Gwen. Theirs was not a Welsh speaking household as her mother could not speak the language but the children were all taught Welsh at school. Ada's mother died when she was 11 and, after leaving school, she went to a secretarial college in Cardiff, where she stayed with two of her aunts who lived there. One of her friends, Meg Foster, then working in a ministry office in Cardiff, asked Ada to join a 'pen pal' group, writing to Polish soldiers stationed in Scotland. Her pen pal was Jerzy Sieczkowski, whom she called George. They later met and, after a brief courtship, were married back in Tontyberen in December 1944. George suffered from health problems following his escape from Poland and so was not sent on active service to France.

After the end of the war, George tried to find out if any of his family had survived. As he could get no information, he and

Ada sadly concluded that all must have perished and decided to put in their application to emigrate to Canada. Then, at the last minute the Red Cross brought him news that his mother was alive. They set off by boat from Ayr in 1947. By this time Ada's father had also died and she and her brother and sister had inherited some money. It was difficult to know what to take with them to Poland so they bought two cars. On arrival they found conditions in Warsaw were as bad for them as for everyone else. Ada and George, his mother and a cousin all lived in one room in Mokotów. They soon realised that they could not afford to run even one of the cars and they were both quickly sold. To make matters worse, Ada then contracted tuberculosis and was sent to a sanatorium in Otwock. There she made a slow recovery but her two months in the sanatorium produced one great benefit: she learned to speak Polish. Ada turned out to be a very quick learner and she later became an excellent Polish speaker, having only the slightest trace of a foreign accent – she claimed that because some sounds in Polish are very similar to Welsh, the language was easier for her. Ada and George's son Janusz was born in 1948 and Ada found a job teaching English at the Methodist School in Plac Zbawiciela. Later, through Jean's help, she was taken on as a translator and proof reader in the Press Summary department of the British Embassy. This job later expanded to include work in the US Embassy. Ada became one of Jean's closest friends but she died of cancer at the age of just 67.

Happily, Betty and Hela are able to tell their own stories about their experiences during the war and after.

Hela Żywiczyńska Boryń's Story
"I was brought up in Inowrocław in Kujawy near Bydgoszcz, about 270 km from Warsaw. After the German invasion in 1939, when I was aged 15, this area was annexed by the Germans and we were all required to report to the Gestapo headquarters every day at 10 o'clock in the morning.

"Then one day, all the young people between the ages of 12

to 15 were rounded up, put on a cattle train, the doors locked, and taken off on a journey. We did not know where we were going. My parents did not know for three months what had happened to me.

"When we got to Berlin, the town was under an Allied bombardment. The train was parked in a siding while the German soldiers ran for cover, but the doors were locked and we could not get out. As the bombing increased, the children started screaming. It was very frightening. When the air raid was over the train made its way though Hamburg to Neumünster in Schlezwig Holstein, near the Danish border.

"We were all taken to a huge hall that was part of a camp where the Germans interned people rounded up from different occupied territories. There were Russians, French, Ukrainians, all sorts. There were a lot of German farmers there who needed labourers to work on their farms. People were being picked out of the crowd by the Germans for their purposes; it was a sort of slave market.

"I was chosen by one of the Germans, and a Polish friend, Stefka Lewczyńska who was twelve at the time, was picked out as well. We were both taken into the countryside and travelled through the forest for about twelve kilometres. It was 15 January 1941 and it was very cold.

"Stefka was then taken to the house of one of the Germans and I was taken to my 'master', who was called Otto. When I got there I met Anna, his wife, and the wife's mother, who was very asthmatic. There were also children, one of whom was born while I was living there. It was a large one storey house and I had a small room with a cement floor; there was no heating and it was very cold. The grandmother, Oma, was a kind woman and took pity on me; she was shocked by how thin I was and used to give me a heated brick from the stove to warm my bed. It was a tough life and when the baby was born, the family were not too worried about the cold as they wanted to 'harden him up'.

"I spent over four years working with the family. I was reasonably well treated; they gave me enough food and I was not abused. My job was to milk the cows, clean the house and do the chores like cleaning and washing up after meals. I had to get up at three o'clock in the morning to go to the fields and milk the cows. There were also five Frenchmen that had been captured from the front and taken to a concentration camp nearby; they were also working on the farm. They were brought in at 6 o'clock each morning and worked until 8 in the evening. After supper they were taken back to the camp.

"The village was occupied by elderly people as all the young ones were in the army and fighting on the German side. Otto also had to go to the German front later on to fight for 'The Fatherland'.

"We often did not sleep at night as we were kept awake by the heavy bombing of Hamburg and the surrounding area. This happened night after night. I remember the noise of the planes coming down overhead. There was one wave after another: bombers circling and dropping bombs, surrounded by fighter planes escorting them. Scarcely had one attack finished before the next one would start. At the end of the raid, the bombers might drop the left-over bombs anywhere so it wasn't safe even in the country.

"Usually we would hear the sirens warning us of an imminent attack. The German wife, Anna, would take the boys to an air raid shelter at the bottom of the garden where the French prisoners of war had dug a bunker.

"After work, the Polish internees in the area used to meet. I used to meet my Polish friends, including Stefka. We all had a large letter on our clothes indicating our country of origin. P for Polen was sewn onto all the clothes we wore: tops, skirts, vests, etc. The Russians had the letter O for Osten (the East). Of course, we depended on the Germans for all our clothes as we had none of our own, but we had to cut out the letters ourselves and then sew them onto our clothes.

"One morning, when I had been in the house for a year, the wife of the German told me that I was not to go to see Stefka after work. I was a defiant teenager and I challenged her. By this time I could speak German quite well so I was able to answer back. Anna said to Otto that she had told me that I was not going to see Stefka that day. Otto said to me, "Why don't you listen to what your mistress is telling you?" I was very angry and I took Otto by the lapels and pushed him; he fell down a few steps. Then I was frightened of the consequences of what I had done, so I rushed upstairs.

"I didn't know what to do but decided that I had to get out of the house. I said I had to go out to get the milk. As I could speak German, I had been able to establish friendly relationships with some of the local people. In particular there was a policewoman who was very friendly to me. She did not have her own children and used to pass sweets to me over the fence. When I went out of the house I ran into this policewoman. She said that Anna had told her that I was unwell and could not come out that day. She obviously did not want to admit that this Polish 'servant' had attacked her husband and provided a different version of events. I told the policewoman what had really happened.

"I stayed on the farm throughout the war. I remember well the liberation day on 8 May 1945. On that day we were liberated by the British. They gave all those whom they found on the farms one week to take revenge on their captors. We could pay back our captors in whatever way we wished - including shooting. I did not choose to do anything of the kind. After a week, normal rules of order returned but the Germans were very nervous and uncertain as to what might happen next.

"With the ending of the war, circumstances were very different: the tables had turned. I stopped milking the cows and was now treated as a 'lady'. Anna, the wife, changed the way she addressed me, using a much more respectful tone. I continued to live with the family and felt obliged to go on helping them with the running of the house, the farm and the cleaning.

"There had been a picture of Hitler, hanging above the desk in the room. About a week after the liberation, I went into the room to do the cleaning as usual. I noticed that the picture of Hitler had disappeared and wondered where it had gone. As I went on with the cleaning I came across the portrait hidden behind a cupboard. I started roaring with laughter and Anna came in and asked me what had happened. It turned out that Anna, becoming uncertain of the outcome of the war, had decided to take Hitler's portrait off the wall and hide it behind the cupboard. She forgot that I would be doing the cleaning. When I explained why I was laughing so much, Anna said to me, "Give me the picture of that dog," and in front of me, she stamped on it, broke the glass and then burnt the portrait. She was ashamed now of having had it in the house.

"I remained on the farm for a month and then had to go to a transit resettlement camp, many of which were created after the war to deal with the thousands of misplaced civilians.

"I did receive some money from the Polish government as compensation for this ordeal. I was given 4200 *złoty* in instalments and the right to free travel. It came fifty years later!"

Stefan Boryń was aged 16 when war broke out and had just completed three years in a *gimnazjum* (secondary school). He joined the underground movement. They used to hold meetings in his home and it was very risky for the whole family. All the papers were in the house and somebody would keep guard during the meetings. Stefan was active in opposition throughout the occupation, which culminated in the heroic but tragic Warsaw uprising of 1944. After the resistance collapsed and the Armja Krajowa was crushed, he was captured by the Germans. Members of the uprising were disarmed, and were interned as prisoners of war. As he had been a soldier, unlike the civilians who ended up in concentration camps, Stefan was taken to a labour camp in Germany and worked in the docks in Hamburg.

By January 1945, several months before the official end of the war, the Germans already knew that the tide of the war was turning against them and they started deserting. Many were high ranking officers: majors, colonels and even generals. Some would stop in the village where Hela lived to hide in the barns.

In a final act of destruction, the Germans began to exterminate their prisoners of war. They marched them to the port near Lubeka where there were old ships moored. Many of them died of illness or exhaustion on the way. They then took shiploads of these prisoners a kilometre or two out to sea from the harbour. The German planes then flew over, bombing the ships, sinking them and killing all the people on board.

Stefan was one of those due to be taken out and killed. His party of prisoners of war had stopped for the night in a village on the way to Lubeka and had slept in a barn. When they woke up, they noticed there were no guards around the barn or in the village. They soon discovered that all the guards had disappeared and that they were now free. It was the morning of 8 May, the day of surrender. A Polish flag was hoisted on top of the barn.

This village was just 7 km from the farm where Hela was, and the two of them met by chance there. The first time he saw her, he told her she would be his wife. They were married the following February in Leizen, 36 km from Hamburg. They lived together for 57 years.

The return to Poland at that time was not straightforward. Stefan was assigned into the 8th British Corps and was fitted out with a British uniform. Hela had to go to a transit resettlement camp. The camp was run on military lines and every morning decisions were announced about who was going to be resettled where. The Poles were nervous about returning to Poland as they were frightened of the Communists, who were establishing control of the country and a new social and political order. Hela was assigned to be transferred to Australia.

The camp was full of people of all nationalities, who were waiting to be sent back to their own countries or elsewhere. It functioned like a little town. There were about 1,000 people in the camp so there was a special need for medical care. The doctors in the resettlement camp looked after all those who had been liberated and Hela was appointed to be a doctor's assistant. There was also a Polish chapel and a chaplain. The Polish chaplain, having the rank of captain, married Stefan and Hela.

One day, about three months after the marriage, a friend of theirs came and said he heard on the radio that Marianna and Jan

Żywiczyńscy were looking for their only daughter. When Hela heard that, she said to Stefan that she did not care about going to Australia any more and that she was going back to Poland. They had to make the decision and risk whatever was awaiting them. Hela was quite clear that whatever the consequences her priority was to see her parents.

They returned to Poland on a ship, the *Queen Mary* to Szczecin. There were 2,500 people taking the same route home. The journey was a scene of utter destruction, wrecks of ships everywhere and also danger of mines which littered the waters and the coast. In Szczecin they were given 100 zł to complete their journey. It was a long way by train through Poznań and they had to change trains to Inowrocław. When she arrived and saw her parents, she had to introduce her husband to them.

Inowrocław is a well known spa; the Germans called it Wartegau. It was not bombed or damaged as the Germans were stationed there during the occupation. But when they got off the tram in the town centre, there were many people standing around asking, "Have you seen so-and-so?" All were hoping for some news of relations and friends who had not returned. On all the houses you would find notices saying "Find me in.... I *am* alive" and the names of people. That was the way people communicated.

Stefan longed to come back to Warsaw. His mother had died from a heart attack in 1940 and his father had disappeared although it is not known whether he died during the bombings of Warsaw or in a concentration camp. But his sister, Irka, had survived the war and Stefan wanted to go back. The house where they had been brought up had been bombed and no longer existed and Irka was staying with her uncle who was a vet in Lublin. Stefan went to Lublin to find her.

Stefan had to register with the army when he came back from Germany as he was still of an age when he could be drafted in. He was still in his British uniform as he had no other clothes to wear.

He was very lucky to be given some good advice. When he went to register he came across an old friend who had been fighting with him during the Warsaw uprising but who had since joined the Communist Party. It was quite common for people to put aside their principles when they were concerned with survival. Stefan had been an officer and his Communist friend told him, "Forget that you were an officer. You are an ordinary soldier and must no longer remember what you have been. Forget your officer's training. You are Stefan Boryń and no more." The alternative was to join the Communist Party, which Stefan, like millions of others, would not contemplate. This Communist friend's advice saved him.

At this time Hela was expecting a baby. When Hania, her daughter, was born, Hela had to go to face a drafting committee to confirm that she was indeed a mother breastfeeding a child and therefore needed her husband to support her. For Stefan this was a way of getting out of the army. Hela had to go to the meeting with a captain from RKU. There was a line of women waiting to prove that they were feeding babies. When Hela's turn came she had to go to a room, take her top off and squeeze her breast to prove that milk was indeed coming out. It was feeding time for Hania so she had no difficulty proving her case. They used to joke for years with Stefan that Hela's 'boobs' saved him from being drafted into the army.

Life in Poland after the war can best be described as 'total poverty'. Anybody that had a flat or house larger than they needed, had to take in somebody who had no accommodation. As large parts of Warsaw had been destroyed that seemed like a practical way out of the problem until the rebuilding of the city started. Hela and Stefan moved into a flat in ulica Ostrobramska, which was occupied by a man who had known Stefan from the uprising. He thought it was better to take in a friend with a family rather than a total stranger. Life was pretty awful. When they got pay at the end of the month they ate well. Before the next pay came in there was little money left and little food. They had to eat anything that was available, horse meat, for example.

As Stefan's education had been interrupted by the war, he had to complete it when the war was over. He trained in librarianship and went to work for a private bookshop. At this stage there were still private enterprises but they were all nationalised later. After the nationalisation he worked in a state-owned bookshop and eventually managed the biggest bookshop in Warsaw.

Hela trained as a librarian and got a job in a military organisation called T1, now called Rawar. The company was making radar systems so it was a sensitive place to work. There was high security and staff screening. All employees had to have passes, even in those days.

Betty McNichol Skwarek's Story

In 1948 Betty Skwarek went back to Edinburgh to see her mother Mrs McNichol. She and her mother were walking down Main Street and she met a friend of Bessie's, who said, "How is your daughter in Poland?" Mrs McNichol replied "This *is* my daughter." Bessie's friend then gave Betty Jean's address in Warsaw. It turned out to be only two streets away from her house and Betty came round to meet her.

Betty had an even more difficult time than Jean on arrival in Warsaw. She lived in Solec, an area of Warsaw near the river which had been badly bombed as it was near the electric power station. A friendship developed. Betty had two children, Stasio, a year older than Wanda and Krysia who was Wanda's age. The four children used to play together every day.

"I met Stanley in Kelso, where I was in the 'Land Army'– I was a 'land girl' in a uniform: you know, breeches and things. I had to do the harvesting and I had to dig up turnips. I didn't like it. I did it for one year and then I met Stanley.

"He had run away from Poland after the German invasion. The war started in September and he and a friend left in November on bicycles. They went to Czechoslovakia and Hungary, somehow he got to Spain and he worked his passage on a Portuguese ship and ended up in Oban. He arrived at Christmas just over a year after he had left home. He was just seventeen. He joined the Polish army when he got to Scotland.

"I was married in Bury St Edmunds where Stanley was stationed. I refused to change my religion but I had to sign papers to say that the children would be brought up as Catholics. He went over to Belgium with his regiment and he was wounded there; he was shot in the foot and the knee. I just got this telegram. They brought him back to Bridgend in Wales and I had to go down there. I was pregnant with Stasio then so my brother came with me. I had no idea what had happened to him but when I found out that he wasn't too bad we just stayed one night there.

"Stasio was just a year and three weeks when Krysia was born. The nurse said to me, "He's a chip off... no she's not, she's a splinter off a Pole!" Then she said, "So he's a Pole, your husband. You'll be back every year!"

"After the war we could have gone to Canada or South America but Stanley wanted to come back; he hadn't seen his mother for seven years. We left from Leith in 1947. He had bought a lorry in Scotland which we brought back with us. We thought it would work but Stanley would never be a businessman and he was young. We had to sell it in the end to get this apartment ready to live in.

"The city had been destroyed; it was just a mass of rubble and conditions were appalling. Any buildings that were left standing were gaping open with ceilings collapsing and toilets hanging from the ruins. There was no glass and window frames had to be filled with plywood. There were no buses; people went by lorry. There were a few shops – not many – but we mostly went to the market. Except we had no money. If you worked in certain jobs you got an allowance of, say, seven kilos of meat for a month – but you had to take it all at once. In the winter you could put it in the gap between the inner and outer windows but in summer it was impossible. Later ration cards were introduced.

"Stanley's father didn't survive the war: he was taken to the concentration camp at Buchenwald. His mother did, but her house had been bombed and she had been given a flat near Solec. This was where we went when we got back to Warsaw. There were two rooms: you went from one into the other. There was a bed – not very big – for Stanley and me and across the room there was Krysia and then there was Kamila and her husband, his brother and his wife – she had a new baby and a girl of five. In the morning I woke up and a woman came through the door from the other room – a big fat woman. And then another woman came out and then a young girl came out and then a boy – it was like a railway station. I said to Stanley, "Who are all these people? He said, "They *live* in there." I said, "I'm not going to lie here with all these people walking in and out". And he said, "Well, you can sleep under the bridge if you like as there's nowhere else." And we were all in the same kitchen and the bathroom. His mother slept in the kitchen – she had a bed in there. Imagine what it was like. Stanley's mother had been left with nothing; I don't know why they told us to come back.

"And I didn't know any Polish either. I learned the hard way. I had to do all my own shopping. One day I wanted to buy a parsnip in the market. I didn't know the word for 'parsnip' but I knew the word for 'carrot' so I asked for a 'big white carrot'. The woman looked a bit puzzled but she worked out what I wanted.

"In the summer I would go to the Vistula with the children. It was a long walk but we would stay there for the whole day. On the way there I used to pass this man in a wee shop and every day he would call to me,"*Dzień dobry, Pani. Gdzie Pani idzie?*" (Good morning, ma'am. Where are you going?) And I would reply, "*Do Wisły*" which I thought meant "To the Vistula" (It should be "*Nad Wisłę*") Every day!

"On the way home in the evening I would pick up a big stick – to protect myself – and then I would break it up and light the fire for the evening meal – even in the heat of summer: there was no other way of cooking. I used to make potato pancakes; fruit soup; milk compote; rhubarb juice; *kopytka* (like dumplings) with meat in sauce.

"The first Easter we were here, we went to church and the priest came round with a crucifix in his hand. I saw everyone kissing it and putting money in the bag. And he said "…pay" And I thought,

"What a country! Here you even have to pay to kiss a crucifix. What he actually said, not very clearly, was, "God will repay you."

"In 1948 I left Stanley at Christmas and went back to Scotland. I was there for three months and my intentions were not to come back here. We knew that Stanley couldn't get a passport to leave Poland but my Mum said to me: "They're not only *your* children, you know. It's a hard life, I know, but go back and try again." So I did. But when I was there in Edinburgh, we met a friend of my Mum and the friend said "Oh, my sister is in Warsaw" and I said, "Whereabouts?" And she said, "I'll let you know" So she phoned and I found out that she lived in Kawcza and I said, "Oh, I'm there every day because I'm living in Ostrobramska and I go to the

Jean, Wanda and Krysia
with Betty Skwarek, 1954

market in Plac Szembeka so I went round to see Jean. I just arrived on the doorstep. Straightaway we became friends: her children were about the same age as mine: Wanda and Krysia were often at our house and my Krysia and Stasio were often at hers.

"Feeding and clothing the children was a real problem. What we had to do was to rip down worn-out garments and put the good bits together to make 'new' ones.

"Then we took this house in Ostrobramska. We paid some money with Stanley's sister and her husband. But it wasn't finished: the walls were just bricks, there were no floors and there were no doors inside the house. So we had the floors put in – all our money went straight away there – and my sister-in-law took one room – the biggest room – and she took what should have been the kitchen and my kitchen was what should have been the bathroom but didn't have any water. We didn't have a toilet for years. The two families lived together for eleven years and we got on great.

"For seven years we had no water and I carried every drop up and every pail down – with two children you can imagine what it was like. The toilet was outside and we had no cess pool. After seven years we put in the water ourselves.

"Jan's mother didn't like me much. She had a long face and she never smiled. She was either knitting or sewing; she wouldn't sit and talk. And she was a bit of a misery; she worked all the time and thought that everyone else should too. "You shouldn't go to the cinema; you shouldn't go anywhere..." Of course we were speaking in English most of the time which she didn't understand. We didn't really know anyone else until Jean went to work in the Embassy. There was Irka from Waszyngtona and a couple of others. I suppose it must have been in the 'fifties that Lady Bertroud used to arrange tea parties at the Embassy for the British-born brides....

"One day I went round to Jean's and I could see that she was terribly upset. She had the bed turned upside down. I said, "What are you doing with that nail brush?" She blurted out between the tears, "I've got bed bugs." They were terrible; they bite and the children were badly bitten. His mother had an ottoman and that's where the bedding was. They were in there, they were in the mattress, they were in all the furniture, even the pictures Jean had brought from Scotland. John managed to get some DDT and we cleaned everything and they were away then. A lot of people in Warsaw had problems like that with so many people living at very close quarters in insanitary conditions. And many had no water. The hygiene was not very good and in the trams and buses, the people were packed together and in summer the smell was appalling.

"We had to make our own entertainment in those days. Of course there was no television; we listened to Radio Free Europe but it was frequently jammed. We played cards: rummy bridge and *tysiąca* (a Polish game). We had one little treat, Jean and I. We used to smoke in those days. We used to go to the shop in the morning and we would buy a packet of five cigarettes and we would unroll the tobacco and roll them up in bits of newspaper. We smoked two and a half cigarettes straight away and that was it for the day. The smell of those cigarettes then: it was awful.

"There was always a celebration on St Andrew's Day in the Embassy and Jean used to do the sword dance in her bare feet with crossed billiard cues for the swords. I think she'd had a few drinks, mind you!

"There were some other Scottish women there: Alice Fronckiewicz and Davina – I forget her other name. When we first came, there were two hundred British wives in Poland but very few of them stayed; most of them went back. Some of the

Jean and Jan with Ada Sieczkowska and Stasio Gierczak

ones that went to homes in the country found themselves living in very primitive conditions like in a farmyard with chickens running around the kitchen with dirt everywhere and barrels of sauerkraut…They couldn't stand that.

"I remember the first time I went back to Britain in 1948, I went on a British plane. It was taking the mail. Krysia was four and Stasio five then. We were sitting there up in the sky and Stasio said, "Mum, where is God's house?" And I said, "Oh, it's further up." It was a poor life and a hard life but we were never stopped from going to church. They say that people were stopped from going to church but that's not true. The people who belonged to the Party, they went on the quiet and they never christened their children. And they talk about these people joining the Party; some people had to - to live. You can't condemn them; they weren't doing anything bad to anyone. We knew some people who were in the Party. They were frightened and they had to have a job somewhere.

"I had friends in Katowice – we came to Poland together – and they said they had this friend – something about difficulty with hotels – could I take him in? I said, "Of course." It must have been in the summer of 1951. This man came on the Saturday and he said he needed to get in touch with the American Embassy but that he had to do it through the British Embassy and would I go there for him? At first I said, "No," but Stanley said there would be no harm so I agreed. He said his name was Paul Greager and that he was working with some newspaper. His story was that he was in the RAF and that they were owed some money which he was supposed to collect.

"I went to the Embassy and gave them the message. "That doesn't sound good. You should have nothing to do with this man – and you mustn't leave the Embassy on foot. We'll phone down to a driver and he will drop you somewhere in the centre of Warsaw."

"A few months later, I came home one evening – it must have been November, anyhow it was dark. I had been giving English lessons. Two men were waiting for me outside the house. "Mrs Elizabeth Skwarek?" "Yes." "We want you to go with us." I said,

"I'm not going anywhere. My children are coming home from school." "You are coming with us." I was a bit frightened so I said, "I shall have to leave the key with my neighbour." "All right but don't say where you are going." I went to my neighbour to ask her. I whispered "UB" (*Urząd Bezpieczeństwa* – the secret police). The neighbour came out after me. "When will you be back?" she called. They replied: "She doesn't know".

"We got as far as the Poniatowski Bridge when they said, "Have you got your ID card?" I said, "No, it's a Monday and I must have left it in my other bag." So we had to go back again to get the key and the ID Card. When we got to our destination he says to me, "Your husband is with us." Hela Boryń had been looking after the children and they had called on her, said they were friends of Stanley's and asked her where he was. She said he is probably fishing and told them where on the Vistula to find him. They asked, "Who was in your house on 22 July?" I said, "I can't remember." They said, "We know who was there."

They kept me there from 4 o'clock to 11 o'clock. There were three of them doing the questioning, in shifts. Then they gave me a rest and brought me a cigarette and some coffee. They seemed to know everything about me – even what we had eaten for dinner. Then they came for me again at 12 o'clock and took me into this big room with a line of men sitting at a long table. They said your

Jean with Hela Boryń and staff in the Pink Club kitchen at the British Embassy

husband is there but you can't speak to him. There was a lot more questioning before they let us go.

"Stanley and I walked all the way home and all the family were waiting for us. Of course the children were six and seven – too young to realise what was going on. I was worried for a whole year after that. Stanley said, "You'll never get out of here again; you'll never get a passport". My heart used to start beating every time I saw a strange car pull up outside the house but I never had any more trouble from them.

"Then they prepared me for giving evidence in court and they were very nice to me... "We want to help you..." We had to go to court for the trial. I had to identify Paul Greager but I was nervous and I pointed at a lawyer by mistake. They were not amused. I got it right the second time. Paul Greager was one of five men sentenced to death for spying.

"I got the job at the English Country Club through Jean. It suited us at the time as we had a better life for the children, accommodation, food and it was a nice place; it was just outside Warsaw. Stasio was 15, Krysia 14. I had to go to have an interview with the Ambassador who told us what the job involved. Stanley was delighted. I was not so keen as I had no experience of catering. It spoilt Stanley and we didn't really take advantage of it as others have before and since: they've bought houses on the proceeds. There were a lot of backhanders and wink-winks going on but that was not my way. I didn't know how to do it. I suppose I could have done it with gloves on. We were there seven years and then I went to be a teacher after that. I didn't like the club: I was away from everyone, I never saw my friends and I had to work evenings and weekends. There were advantages: we had a more comfortable life and we were able to buy food from the shop – up to £5 I think it was – chocolate and things that we couldn't get anywhere else.

"So we left the club and Krysia wanted to go to Scotland and get a job but her English was very, very poor. I took her to a shop in Bridges to see if she could get a job as a shop assistant. The manager said to me, "I don't want to talk to you; I want to talk to your daughter." So he did and then he said, "Yes, we'll train her up for a couple of weeks and see how it goes." They put her downstairs in the basement with the china; then they moved her upstairs to hosiery. Meanwhile I got a job in the cash department. In those days there was a system that when the customer paid, the cash was put into a kind of box which was sent by an overhead wire to the cash desk. The cashier took the money, put the change in the box and sent it zooming back. Well, I was the cashier. I was there for three months and then I came back to Poland.

"And I had this idea of teaching English so I went round to this school when it was closed and I spoke to some people there and they said, "Yes, of course we can find a job for you." So I said, "I've had no training; could I go into a class to see?" So I did and I took the job. It was my eighth lesson when they said they were sending in two people to observe me. So I said to the children, "I want you to be very good today – you're always good, but I want you to be especially good as we've got visitors coming," and I could see they thought the visitors were coming to see them. The lesson went very well: it was for beginners: "What is this? The pencil is on the table. What colour is the pencil?", that sort of thing. The lesson went very well and they paid me more money after that. Of course I didn't have any papers or anything but I went on doing it for sixteen years and I liked it. I like children. I never had very good marks for English at school – I had better marks for French – but I seemed to get on all right.

"Stanley became a driver for the Ambassador at the Iranian Embassy and then he got a job at the Bristol (Hotel). By this time Krysia was 21 and Stasio was married."

Sadly George Sieczkowski passed away in 1995, Stanley Skwarek in 1996 and Stefan Boryń in 2003. Hania Boryń married a Pole, has three children and lives in Chicago. Krysia Skwarek married a Pole, has one child and lives in Edinburgh. Stasio Skwarek married a Pole has two children and lives in Warsaw.

12

Better Times: The Pink Club

JEAN: "BY 1958, THE CHILDREN were teenagers and I was looking for a job. I thought of going back to nursing but the language was a problem. With Hela and Betty, I went up to Kasprzaka, a factory that made electric bulbs or something, but they wouldn't take us on. Then I got this introduction to the British Embassy in Aleja Róż. They said they were looking for someone to cook. I said, "I've been trained as a nurse; I'm not a cook. So they said, "Never mind; we'll train you". So I was put to work for Pani Bronisława, a real old maid and a staunch Catholic, who had been in a Nazi concentration camp during the war. After her retirement, Pani Stefańska took over. I learnt how to cook from them and after a couple of years, they asked me to manage the club. I had Valeria, then Maryla as cleaners and waitresses, and Pani Zosia who washed up. It was quite hard work: I would get in there before 7 am and there were always a few people who came in for breakfast. Some would rush in at five to nine and require something instantly. Then we would prepare lunch which was a full three-course meal. Most of the Embassy staff had lunch and there was also a group of regulars from the Indian Embassy next door. I finished at 2 pm but was back at 5 pm until 11 pm.

"Any occasion or anniversary was an excuse for a celebration: Burns' Night – haggis, tatties 'n neeps – St Andrew's Day, St Patrick's Day, Hallowe'en, when I would dress up as a witch – toffee apples and treacle – or it might be a visiting party: The Royal Shakespeare Company,

National Philharmonic Orchestra, or the ice show, Holiday on Ice; Lulu came once. The Scottish evenings, when I used to decorate the club with tartan rugs and we had a piper in from the Canadian Embassy, were particularly riotous. A popular drink comprised whiskey, honey and barley, mixed with a silver – it had to be silver – spoon.

Special days such as the Queen's Birthday would often warrant a party in the Ambassador's Residence in Ulica Bagatela, but Jean would usually be pulled in to do the catering.

It must be unusual for the manager of a social club to be awarded the MBE, but then Jean was rather an unusual person. British people, especially when they first arrived, would often feel acutely uncomfortable in Poland. From the moment they set foot in the airport, they were made to feel unwelcome by surly officials. Visitors' possessions were minutely recorded at the airport, not because they might be bringing in illegal goods, but so that nothing could be taken out of the country on departure later. The close presence of uniformed, armed guards contributed to the generally threatening atmosphere.

Hallowe'en at the Pink Club, 1972: Jean and Maryla

All visitors had to exchange a certain amount of foreign currency for złotys at the 'official rate' and motorists had the added imposition of having to buy fuel at an absurdly inflated price. The language was often a problem and, unlike Western Europe, the public and road signs were incomprehensible.

Of course, if you were fortunate enough to know some Polish people, that feeling would be dispelled in a moment as there are no more generous people in the world – and that was especially true when deprivation was so acute that they had very little to offer. But many people did not know any Poles and to them Jean was a godsend. If you didn't know the answer to some local problem, it was always, "Go and see Jean in the Pink. She'll help you." Her father had told her as a child that we are on this earth to help other people and Jean has followed that maxim all her life – and derived great pleasure from doing so.

The cliché, "it's a small world" is much overused but I think indulgence might be exercised in the case of Ronnie and Betty MacLean. Ronnie MacLean was in Warsaw from 1968-70 as a United Nations Technical Assistant when he was International Director of the Potassium Exploration Project. The excuse was, he says, to look for potash deposits in Poland; in reality, its main function was to update Polish geophysicists, whose direction from the Soviet Union was in outdated techniques with obsolete equipment.

On arrival in Warsaw, Ronnie and Betty, having presented themselves at the British Embassy and signed the visitors' book as was the practice, were invited to a reception at the Ambassador's residence. They were greeted by a member of the embassy staff: "Ah, you're from Scotland. Have you met Jean yet? She's from Ailsa Craig."

As it happened, Jean's 82 year-old mother was paying her first and only visit to Poland at the time and she and Betty MacLean were introduced. When Betty had overcome her understandable incredulity that anyone could have been born on that inhospitable rock, the conversation continued:

"So your husband was a lighthouse keeper, Mrs Clark. Have you heard of Rubha nan Gall?"

"Indeed I have – I lived there for five years and my grandchildren were born in the house."

"Gracious! We are from Tobermory and we knew well the MacMillans." (Mr MacMillan was the keeper before John Clark. Nurse MacMillan, the midwife that delivered the Clark granddaughters, was his sister.)

"What was your maiden name, Mrs MacLean?"

"Spink."

"Oh, you must be Mr Spink the lawyer's daughter. I knew your parents and your sister Jean and brother Duncan, but I don't think we have met."

"No, indeed! We knew that one of your daughters had married a Pole. It caused quite a stir on the island that a daughter of the Master of the Freemasons' Lodge had married a Roman Catholic. "Give it two years," they said!"

The Tobermory connection created a close bond between Betty MacLean and Jean. Betty used to play bridge in the Pink Club every Monday, and Jean and Jan were frequently called upon when the MacLeans were entertaining at home. Betty MacLean was a good cook herself and always insisted on preparing the meal, but she was grateful for help in presentation, serving and waiting. Needless to say, Ronnie and Betty were enthusiastic participants in the Burns Night celebrations, commenting that it was more 'Scottish' than they would have had at home. She and Jean kept up a regular correspondence until Betty's death in 2005, and they met again when Ronnie and Betty made a return visit to Poland in 1997."

There must have been many stories of Jean coming to the rescue of 'lost' Westerners, but a couple will suffice.

Jean: "I was working at the Embassy at the time and I had just got off the tram at Plac Szembeka when I saw this motorbike and sidecar with GB plates, parked by the side of the road. GB plates in Warsaw at that time were extremely rare – especially in the suburbs. I went back to the flat, left my bag and shopping and went to see who it belonged to. I saw them straight away, a man, a woman and two girls aged about 11 and 12. I think the girls were red-haired, anyhow they were clearly not Poles. So I said to the woman in English, "Can I help you?" She said that she was looking for a cup of tea. So I said, "Well, you won't get a cup of tea here. You'd better come along with me."

It turned out that the wife was Polish and the husband Welsh. The wife had been taken as a 16-year-old to Germany to work on the land and he had been stationed in Germany when they met. They went back to live in the UK but she had left family in the east of Poland that she had not seen for nearly twenty years. He was determined to take her back but they had little money and so the family of four had set off into the unknown on this motorbike and sidecar. On the way back the bike had broken down just outside Warsaw and they had pushed it into the town. They had taken it into a garage for repairs and were planning to go to the British Embassy for advice on accommodation. Jean was able to advise them that the Embassy closed at 5 o'clock and invited them to stay the night in her flat. The next morning they picked up the bike and set off for the coast in something of a hurry as their visas had very little time before expiry – a solecism that Polish officials were unlikely to treat with indulgence. The wretched bike broke down again and this time Jean was able to direct them to a mechanic. Fitted out with spare parts and back on the road they made the ferry by the deadline – just. Back in the UK, the husband wrote a book on it in which he expressed his gratitude to Jean, and sent her a copy. For many years they kept up a correspondence and sent photographs.

Jean again: "There was this woman from Szczecin, who arrived in the British Embassy one morning. She had come to Poland with her husband, who had taken her back to live on his farm. Life turned out to be rather different to what she had expected. Because she wouldn't – or couldn't – milk the cows, her mother-in-law had made her live in a pigsty. She and her two children had then run away from the farm and the mother had been working in the fields to earn the money to pay her fare up to Warsaw. She wanted to get back to Glasgow and was asking the Embassy to help her.

"The Consul said to me, "Jean, give her a good meal and charge it to the Pink Club". So I did that and I told her that if she wanted to stay the night I could put her up. Betty Skwarek came round in the evening and brought some clothes and we gave her a good meal and dressed her up. Before she went she said, "Jean after what you've done for me, I'm going to get you out of this country. It's not fit to live in!" Eventually she got onto a boat from Szczecin but I never heard from her again."

Ian Chalmers was the Cultural Secretary at the Embassy from 1970 to 1972.

"The Pink Club in the British Embassy in Warsaw was the focus for all visiting Britons. There was nowhere where anyone could get a decent meal in those days and 'The Pink' provided not only a first class restaurant but also an atmosphere well distanced from all that awful Communist security. Foreign Office inspectors who turned up at the Embassy every now and again used to tell me that the British Embassy in Warsaw was the happiest in the world. One thing was that there was no hierarchy. Every one met on the same terms and business men and blue collar workers were as welcome as diplomats from other embassies like the Indian and Canadian. As well as the restaurant and bar there were dances and bingo and all sorts of escapes from the austerity of 1970s Poland.

"It fell to me to be secretary of The Pink Club so I saw Jean in action at close quarters. She operated with great efficiency and much charm.

"In those days Poland had close ties with the UK Amateur Athletic Association and athletes used to visit frequently. One day a party of about thirty came over and we gave a bash for them at our house. Jean came to prepare the buffet for us but was not used to athletes' appetites. I saw what she had got in and suggested that she bought another three of those huge tins of ham we used to get. She thought that this was quite ridiculous but reluctantly agreed. When she saw the guests piling their plates like pyramids, she realised what I meant. We just got away with it but there was very little left over at the end of the evening.

"Jean was a larger than life character who combined the qualities of being the life and soul of the party with being completely unflappable. She always had her feet firmly planted on the ground."

Of course, the traffic in kindness was not all one way. Many people at the Embassy were very kind to Jean too and small kindnesses could make a huge difference to lives hamstrung by bureaucratic obstructions and obfuscations. In the really bad days – the Stalinist period – she had been unable to get a passport to her father's funeral: certain things were not possible. But many people at the embassy went out of their way to be helpful.

An Irishman, Mr Macalinden, whose reputation lives on for poisoning most of the embassy staff after a feast of lamb and oysters at a notoriously riotous St Patrick's Day party, arranged for Jean's salary to be sent to her mother in Scotland for one month in three – which among other things enabled her mother to visit Warsaw in 1970. Another dodge was for the embassy to pay staff in cigarettes and whiskey – two very valuable commodities in Poland at that time. Duty free, they cost the embassy very little, but for the recipients they could be sold on the black market to considerable advantage.

On the occasion of Jean and Jan's silver wedding anniversary in 1968, they paid for her and the children to travel to Britain (not Jan as well of course: one member of the family always had to stay behind to prevent an 'escape'). They also presented her with a silver canteen of cutlery.

The MBE awarded to Jean in June 1978 was recognition of the service she had given, not only to diplomats and embassy staff, but also to the many 'lost souls' that had run aground in Warsaw during the communist period. It was presented to her by the Ambassador at the time, Kenneth Bridham. Even that was not without its complications: by marrying a Pole and going to live in Poland, Jean had not only given up her home, her family and her religion; she had forfeited her British nationality. It was therefore necessary for both governments to give their approval for the award. Even the Polish government on this occasion was gracious enough to do so.

Jean receiving her MBE from the British Ambassador to Poland, His Excellency Kenneth Bridham, June 1978

It may seem odd to the reader that someone running a small social club in a country far from home should receive such a distinction. I asked Ronnie MacLean why he thought this happened.

Ronnie MacLean: "Jean's position may have been Manager of the Pink Club but she was very much more than that. Her cross-cultural knowledge and her canny awareness of how to deal with Poles made her the focal point for Brits and other Westerners in need of wise counsel. In addition, her innate charm and the affection in which she was held, led to a call for recognition from generations of diplomats, delegates and business people that had passed through Warsaw in the preceding twenty years."

Jean retired from The Pink Club in 1981.

Meanwhile Wanda and Krysia had been to school in Warsaw, Wanda starting in 1951 and Krysia a year later. Both went to the local primary school, a one storey house now occupied by flats, just two streets away from their house.

Krysia: "In the devastated and impoverished Poland after the war, education was one way of improving your lot, so there was a healthy emphasis on learning and a generally positive attitude to school. Everyone was poor – and the communist system insisted on equality according to Marxist and Leninist dogma – but education was an opportunity to attain professional status if not to improve your material position.

"Opportunities of extra curricular activities in the primary school were very limited. In the small garden yard of the school, there were athletics competitions such as high jump or long jump, but only those activities which did not require any special facilities or equipment. There were no tennis courts or swimming pools. Such luxuries were not available in a city which still lacked adequate basic living accommodation."

Just like in Blair's Britain of 2007, in addition to secondary schools (*Liceum Ogólnokształcące*), there were 'specialist academies'. At the age of 13, Wanda went to *Technikum Gastronimiczne,* a school specialising in Domestic Economy and Krysia to *Technikum Księgarskie* which was a specialist school for Librarianship. Again the education was good: there was a broad curriculum and many dedicated teachers who, like elsewhere, joined the profession out of idealism and enthusiasm for their subject. The pupils studied a broad range of subjects and took their final exams (*matura*) in around eight subjects at the age of 18.

Unfortunately schools and universities were also politicised and the official version of history and politics was taught to make sure all pupils and students knew the communist countries' version of the past. The indoctrination of young minds was too good an opportunity to miss. Every classroom in every school had three pictures on those walls, those of Marx, Lenin and Stalin. Young children were taught about the father figure, Jósef Stalin, and would learn the story of his life and about his friendship to Poland. One day in March 1953, Krysia came home from school in tears; it turned out to be because of the announcement that Stalin had died.

Russian was a compulsory subject in both primary and secondary school unless pupils chose another language. Because the majority of Poles saw the Russians as oppressors, there was an understandably negative attitude to learning the language. In spite of several years of learning, neither Wanda nor Krysia could speak or write more than a few words of Russian.

Excellence in sports was good for the image of the Eastern Block, so sport was encouraged even if the facilities were woeful. When Krysia went to secondary school she used to travel halfway across Warsaw to a swimming pool, but opportunities for learning music, singing or art were limited. It was partly to do with the shortage of trained teachers but also lack of musical instruments, lack of paints, brushes and other essential equipment.

Jan and Jean at the garden party to celebrate the Queen's birthday at the Ambassador's Residence, 1979

13

The Secret Police and the Church

"THERE CAN BE FEW COUNTRIES in the world where the system of government is held in greater disrepute than it is in Poland." – Norman Davies.

One of the least attractive features of life under this universally loathed regime was the secret police – in Poland the *Urząd Bezpieczeństwa* (Bureau of Security) – and the use of informers. This led to an all-pervading atmosphere that varied from suspicion to downright terror. Everywhere there were stories of somebody being taken in or someone being followed. As nobody quite knew who was working for the UB, nobody outside one's closest family could be trusted. Just recently files from the communist period have been made available to the public and have produced some very unpleasant surprises: best friends, close confidants, even husbands and wives have all been found to have been working for UB. There are some suspicions that are too sensitive even to mention in this story.

Betty Skwarek has already told the story of Paul Greager. From the safety of the passage of fifty years, the full impact of that incident, and others like it, have become blurred. The plain fact is that Paul Greager, or whatever his real name may have been, was executed: shot or hanged. This was shocking and the UB made sure that everyone knew about it, keeping the atmosphere of fear bubbling.

'Ex-pat Brits' were always under suspicion, with their Western connections, but they were also potentially very useful if they could be persuaded to compromise their principles – and some were. Later when Jean managed the Pink Club in the British

Embassy and Krysia used to give Polish lessons to some of the diplomats, they frequently came under pressure.

Krysia: "One day, quite out of the blue, I received a letter from the Ministry of Internal Affairs (*Ministerstwo Spraw Wewnętrznych*) asking me to come for an interview at Room 156 at the Ministry in Ulica Rakowiecka. At first I was surprised as I had had no previous contacts with the Ministry and the letter gave no reason for the meeting. The address, however, was ominous. The Ministry had a reputation in Warsaw and we used to use the phrase, "to be invited to Ulica Rakowiecka" as a code for being in trouble with the Party.

"At the time I had contacts with a number of people in the British Embassy: I was giving Polish conversation lessons to two of the Cultural Secretaries, and I was also teaching the children of some other diplomats. I had visited their homes and had been invited to parties by them. Also I was Jean's daughter and she knew everybody in the Embassy – so the call was not that much of a surprise, really.

"In preparation for the interview I told myself that I had to stick to some basic rules: I was determined to appear calm, and not to get drawn into any detailed conversations. I was also aware that some traps might be set for me. It was well known that providing information, however insignificant, might bring benefits: jobs could become easier to get, housing difficulties could melt away, and useful interventions could be made to ease passport applications. These were benefits that could be very tempting.

"When I arrived at the Ministry, it was clear that I was expected. I was ushered to Room 156. On entering, I was astonished to see that the person sitting in the office waiting for me was a man I knew well by sight. He was a little older than me – in his early thirties – but he had grown up and lived in the next street. I remembered him as a teenager who used to hang out with his mates in the street near the market.

"He behaved throughout the interview as if he had never seen me before in his life. This was quite unnerving as he clearly knew a great deal about me. All homes of British diplomats were under constant surveillance, so it was no surprise that they knew about my comings and goings. He reeled off the names of all the people that I knew and had details of all my visits to their houses and the Embassy.

"What did surprise me was his line of questioning, as he seemed mainly interested in specific individuals that I did not know that well. I can only presume that they were involved in activities that were of especial importance to the Party. There I genuinely couldn't help him. He wanted to know more details about my conversations with particular people, but also strongly hinted that he would welcome any more information that my contacts would enable me to provide for him.

"I steered a simple line by saying that my main interest was in teaching Polish to earn some pocket money and to get some exposure to English conversation, the language I was studying. I agreed that I was sometimes invited to parties in their houses but insisted that I saw these as merely another opportunity to practise my English. That was, of course, not strictly true as I enjoyed these contacts and was able to be in surroundings off limits to most Polish people.

"He concluded the interview by asking me to get in touch with him if I had any information that I wished to share with him. I replied in a polite but non-committal way. I suppose it was an invitation to me to collaborate; it could also have been interpreted as 'a shot across the bows'."

One day a stranger approached Jan on the bus and told him he wanted to meet him for a coffee. He gave a date, time and place. Jan did not go to the meeting. The following day, the same man turned up at the house, asked Jean to leave so that he and Jan could speak, and told Jan that they wanted him to collect information from the British Embassy. Jan told the man that he worked as a gardener at the Ambassador's residence: he had no access to any information that could possibly be of use to them. The man left, far from pleased.

A few nights later, Jan was returning from an evening at the Dutch Embassy where he had been a guest at a celebration of an anniversary of the liberation of Breda. He later had little recollection of the encounter but the facts seem to be that he was pounced upon at a corner near the house, hit on the head, spectacles broken, his ring, watch and wallet were taken and he spent two weeks recovering in hospital. The Dutch Embassy sent a message of sympathy and a hamper of fruit; Jan also had a message from the UB to let him know they were aware of the incident.

Ronnie MacLean says that it was well known that office and private telephones were bugged. He knew of a number to dial to test whether his call would be picked up. He was also aware that his administrative assistant was regularly photocopying all his documents. And, of course, the intelligence business was two-way: many diplomats and foreigners **were** involved in spying at one level or another.

Krysia and I had a very mild experience of their activities on one of our visits to Warsaw in the 1970s. Her cousin Andrzej had very generously decided to take the family out to dinner at a restaurant. At the time, this was an almost unheard of treat; apart from anything else, the cost to him of the evening was equal to a month's salary (although such was the rate of exchange on the black market that I could have paid for it all with a ten pound note). There was only one other couple in the restaurant, sitting rather oddly – as the room was otherwise empty - a table or two away. Having made our selection from the menu – not difficult as only one dish from the fairly long list was available – we settled to a glass of beer, the wine being prohibitively expensive and also undrinkable. We noticed that the other couple were taking little interest in each other – indeed their body language suggested their relationship was business rather than romantic – but made no comment until we had left the restaurant. The Poles among us were all aware who our neighbours had been: UB; and they had been listening to our conversation and recording it using a bug under our table. It was yet another example, not only of the futile waste of resources but also of the creation of an atmosphere where Big Brother is always looking over your shoulder. Like the poor, the UB were always with us. A recent film, *The Lives of Others,* told a story of a similar situation in the former East Germany.

The relationship between the Church and the State in Poland during the communist period has been the subject of complete books. What was so fascinating was that it was the obverse of the situation in the UK where the Church of England is inextricably linked with the State, but few of the population are practising members; in Communist Poland the Roman Catholic Church had no official status but 95% of the population were practising members. Indeed the Church played a big part in the downfall of communism – accelerated by the election of the Polish Pope, Karol Wojtyła. Although religion was not officially recognised by the state, people's lives were guided by religious beliefs and values.

Norman Davies again: "The state was officially godless, and gave no support to organised religion. In the resulting struggle, every citizen was caught in a welter of divided loyalties which he had to reconcile as best he could. Split minds, double lives and double think were the order of the day. It was not unusual for young priests to be anti-clerical, for example, or for communists to be church-goers. Workers were often required on pain of dismissal to attend factory meetings or political rallies carefully arranged to clash with religious demonstrations. Somehow, with candle in one pocket and red flag in the other, they contrived to attend, and be late for, both. School children, sent on an obligatory free excursion to the mountains, learned that their home town lay on the route of a visiting cardinal. Their coach-driver, like the good Catholic he was, would see that they returned home early in order to cheer His Reverence (whose visit was the cause of their excursion in the first place)...Few people bothered to denounce the state ideology openly; all too many, in the eyes of the clergy, attended church as a matter of habit and social tradition, or merely as an assertion of their right to a life of their own."

It is a fascinating topic but one that does not concern us here, beyond the way that it affected Jean, her family and friends, and how it affected everyday life in Poland.

Jean, although she had been a member of the Free Church of Scotland – a Presbyterian – had not been a practising church-goer. Before she could marry Jan, she had been obliged to convert to Roman Catholicism, which had involved attending catechism classes. The Presbyterians, as we have seen earlier, were no lovers of 'popery' and her parents would have been at least exposed to sectarian hatred in their Glaswegian upbringing. Bessie's refusal to attend the wedding illustrates the point. So it was a brave decision but a sensible one, if they were going to return to Poland.

However Jean's brief introduction to Catholicism in Edinburgh would have given her little insight into the Polish version which has a history and momentum all of its own, and is heavily overlaid with patriotism. It must have been another shocking cultural experience.

Jean accepted – if not exactly embraced – Catholicism, and fell in line with the practices of the family and the local people. Although there was no religious education in schools, Wanda and Krysia went to religious classes in the local church of Marji Niepokalanego Serca near Plac Szembeka. The festivals were celebrated according to the Polish Catholic tradition: they attended midnight mass at *Wigilia* (Christmas Eve), when consecrated wafers were shared to symbolise the body of Christ, born at Christmas. At Easter they would take painted eggs and bread to the local church to be blessed on Easter Saturday. And of course, baptisms, first communions, marriages and funerals were all conducted in accordance with the rites of the Church.

Jan and Jean in the Old Town, Warsaw, with Mr and Mrs McBain, visitors from Britain

14
Wanda and Krysia

WANDA TOOK HER MATRICULATION AND left school in 1961. She decided that she had had enough of studying and did not want to go on to University, so she began to look for a job. By that stage she had already met Krzysztof, whom she was later to marry, and it was through Krzysztof's father – everything being done by networking, of course – that she got a job, book-keeping in a small business.

In 1964, by which time Poland was under the Government of Władysław Gomułka (1956–1970), Jean, Wanda and Krysia made a second visit to Britain. Again Jan was obliged to stay behind. They stayed with Jean's brother, Ian and Mary, who were very kind to them, and took them on holiday to Looe in Devon. Unfortunately Jean contracted jaundice but Wanda and Krysia went to Kidderminster to meet Jan's great friend, Kocjan and his wife Lidia. Kocjan had stayed in Britain after the war. Then they went on to Bessie's in Musselburgh. Wanda was now 20 and Krysia 19, both extremely beautiful young ladies.

One of the ideas associated with this visit was that Wanda might find a job in Britain, an idea that foundered on two obstacles: first, she didn't really speak English well enough to get a job with close contact with people – washing-up could not really be described as a 'career opportunity' – and second and far more importantly, such a scheme would mean a lengthy separation from Krzysztof. Clearly out of the question. On the other hand the visit made a definite impression on Krysia, who, from this time, set her heart on a life in Britain.

Krzysztof was initially working as a teacher but he had a

keen interest in gliding and spent most of his free time at a small airfield, Lotnisko Gocławskie, just across the fields leading to the river Wisła, not far form Jean's house. Wanda used to spend every moment she could find with him and eventually got her own gliding certificate.

Krzysztof moved from gliders to aeroplanes and set about accumulating flying hours in order to get a pilot's licence; that meant the pair had even more reason to be at the airfield. One advantage of living in the communist system was that the use of the airfield facilities and training were free. Wanda and Krzysztof were married in 1967 and had two children: Marysia in 1971 and Michał in 1980.

As a qualified pilot, Krzysztof had managed to get a job with the Polish national airline, LOT. Polish pilots were not paid well in those days – they scraped a living like everybody else – but the job did open up opportunities of going abroad. This enabled him to save his allocation of expenses and occasionally bring home goods that could not be bought in Poland. So, life for them was marginally better than for the rest.

There was strict control over people going abroad. He knew

Above left: Jean, Wanda and Krysia with June, Ian's wife Mary, and Bessie

Above right: Jean with Wanda and Krysia on Jean's first return visit to Scotland, 1955

that on every flight, there would be somebody who would be watching the crew. It would probably be one of the staff but nobody quite knew who. Contacts with anybody abroad were out of the question if a pilot or an air hostess wanted to keep their job. Krzysztof maintained that no-contact behaviour even after the fall of communism and would never contact friends or family when he flew into London. It was safer to be careful.

When Krysia started studying English at school, she found that she could recall little of the language that had been her first language as a child. However, many words and sounds were very familiar, so it did not take her long to pick it up again. A dose of British culture on her visit in 1955 had provided a boost to her interest and she duly won a place to study English Philology at Warsaw University in 1964. She took full advantage of this opportunity and threw herself into academic life. Studying English gave her a reason for going to the British Council library in Aleje Jerozolimskie or the American Embassy library to find books otherwise unavailable anywhere else in Warsaw. After finishing her university course in 1969, Krysia qualified as a teacher of English and initially taught in a secondary school, *Liceum Ogólnokształcące*, near ulica Wiatraczna.

In 1970 Isabella Clark, Jean's mother, made the momentous decision to visit Jean in Warsaw. Although she was no stranger to sea travel, she had never flown before, but, at the age of 82, she made her maiden flight, stopping in Berlin on the way. She stayed in Poland for three months and by all accounts the visit was a great success. Wanda and Krysia took her all over Warsaw, to the theatre and the opera – which she appeared to enjoy with the help of her able interpreter; everyone made a great fuss of her. The Embassy staff were also very kind to her, and invited her to cocktail parties and other events. June and July can be very hot in Warsaw and loose, light clothing is essential for comfort. Granny Clark however had worn a corset all her life – she even presented Jean with a corset immediately after Wanda was born. Now was not the time to break the habit of a lifetime and she steadfastly refused to remove her corset as the temperatures soared.

By 1972 there was relaxation of the strict rules about travelling abroad and the Polish authorities granted Krysia a passport to the UK to see her family.

Krysia: "I had one great advantage and that was the fact that I had been born in Scotland. Although I had a Polish passport, as far as the British were concerned, I was a British subject and had

Wanda and Krzysztof on their wedding day

dual nationality. I would have no difficulties entering the country – I wouldn't even need a visa.

"This was a stroke of extraordinary good fortune. It seemed that life there was full of opportunities. First of all, there was freedom. Nobody can quite appreciate what that means unless they are deprived of it. You could say what you thought, think what you wanted, read what you chose and life seemed based on sensible principles of individual choice and tolerance. I knew that if the opportunity of staying permanently in the UK presented itself I would take it and not consider returning to Poland.

"First, I got a clerical job in the Bank of Scotland – it seemed a logical place to start given my background. Then I moved to an administrative position with Frederick Warne, a small family publishing firm which had had the good fortune to have as one of its clients Beatrix Potter – she of Peter Rabbit fame. There was clearly no future with such a firm, but it enabled me to find my feet in a country where many customs were still strange. At the time I was staying with my childhood friend, Hania from Kawcza, who had also come over to England: in her case as an au pair at the house of the Head Master of Harrow School. There she had met and married a young teacher at the school, George Attenborough. It was while staying with them that I met and later married Dale, also a master at Harrow School. I could not have entered a world more different from the communist system in which I had been brought up."

As Dale had been married previously, the wedding was conducted at the Civic Centre in Harrow, an unlovely building all too reminiscent of the architecture of post-war Warsaw – at least the Polish guests felt at home. This was followed by a blessing by the Chaplain in the Harrow School Chapel, the greatest concession the Church was prepared to make, according to its rules at the time. Jean and Jan were present and the reception was held in the Old Harrovian Room at the School. The year was 1976.

Although the iron grip on the people was easing slightly during the decade of Edward Gierek's period as First Secretary (1970-80), life in Poland was still extremely hard. The political struggle which would culminate in the emergence of Solidarity and the subsequent period of martial law was another very difficult time for all Poles. Food was rationed and prices rose dramatically. Such basic commodities as sugar, tea, coffee or toilet paper were just not available. Shops were empty and often closed, as they had nothing to sell. The news of an imminent delivery spread rapidly by word of mouth and queues would start forming. Although the British Embassy provided a lifeline, Jean had to struggle like everybody else to get essential food supplies. She would stand in queues for hours outside shops in the hope that a delivery would be made.

However, support was also possible from overseas by now. There were many Poles living in the UK with beleaguered families in Poland and companies sprang up, specialising in deliveries of parcels by lorry. Krysia took advantage of the bargains available in jumble sales and charity shops at the time and bought suitable items for members of the family: skirts, jumpers, coats or jackets. She also sent tins of food and other non-perishables, still unobtainable in Poland at the time.

*Jan, Krysia, Wanda, Stasio Skwarek, and Krzysztof's parents
at Marysia's Christening*

15
A Time of Turmoil: Solidarity

Norman Davies: "During the ten years which separated the summer of 1980 from the autumn of 1990, Poland experienced a political roller-coaster ride, such as few countries have ever endured. At the start of the decade, she was still in the grip of communist dictatorship and the Soviet Bloc. At the end, she was a free nation. There were three distinct phases. In 1980-81, the independent Solidarity Movement – the only independent organisation of its kind in the history of the Soviet Bloc – mounted an unprecedented challenge to the ruling Party's monopoly. In 1981-83, the military element within the communist system launched a violent counter-attack, introducing martial law, suppressing all overt Solidarity activities and desperately trying to impress its Soviet masters. From 1983-90, the military leaders failed in all their attempts to restore a viable Communist order, eventually choosing to reinstate Solidarity and to aim for stability through partnership. The outcome was the opposite of that intended. The communist system collapsed."

In November 1981, Jean and Jan came to London for the birth of Krysia's baby. It was possible for them to leave the country together as Wanda and the rest of the family were staying behind. Ashley arrived safely on 11 November and the arrangement was that Jan would return to Warsaw on 12 December but that Jean would stay for a while to help Krysia with the baby. Martial Law (*stan wojenny*) was declared on 13 December.

Wanda: "It was a Sunday and I woke up early as usual. Krzysztof had flown off to Romania so I was spending the day on my own with the children. At some stage in the morning I put on the television and was surprised that there was no picture. I tried to make a telephone call but the line was dead. I then looked out of the window and saw tanks and soldiers in the street. A while later, the picture came on the television screen and General Jaruzelski was broadcasting to the nation that there was a state of emergency. It was all very frightening."

The period that followed was one of great uncertainty for the family and for Poles in general. For Jean in England, the immediate aftermath was very worrying: all communications to and from Poland had been cut off and there was no means of contacting anybody. Information on BBC news bulletins was sporadic and non-specific. Krzysztof was grounded in Romania and Wanda did not know when he was going to be able to return. When at last

Jean and Jan at home, 1988

he came back and was able to resume flights, he managed to post a letter in Switzerland to Jean in London: it was a letter from Jan saying he and the family were all right. When the borders eventually reopened, Jean returned to Warsaw.

Of course, this crisis had not come out of the blue. Lech Wałęsa's name first came to public notice in 1970 when he was a member of an illegal strike committee in Gdańsk Shipyard. Riot police had moved in; more than 80 workers were killed; Wałęsa was arrested, convicted of 'anti-social behaviour' and spent a year in prison. In 1976, Wałęsa was dismissed from his job in Gdańsk Shipyard for collecting signatures for a petition to build a memorial for the killed workers, but he sensed the groundswell of support and, in 1978, he and some colleagues formed the illegal underground Free Trade Union of Pomerania (*Wolne Związki Zawodowe Wybrzeża*). He was arrested several times in 1979 for organising anti-state activities, but not convicted of any offence.

On August 14, 1980, at the beginning of another strike in the Lenin Shipyard, Wałęsa, in an orchestrated and much publicised act, scaled the shipyard wall. This was a signal for a general strike across the country. In September of that year, the Communist government signed an agreement with the Strike Coordination Committee to allow legal organisations, but not actual free trade unions. The Strike Coordination Committee re-invented itself as the National Coordination Committee of *Solidarność* Free Trade Union, and Wałęsa was chosen as chairman of this Committee. By now the Solidarity movement was starting to gain popularity, both within Poland and abroad. He kept this position until December 11, 1981, when he was arrested. Martial law was declared two days later and Wałęsa interned for eleven months in south-eastern Poland, near the Soviet border.

General Wojciech Jaruzelski became the Communist Party's National Secretary and Prime Minister, positions he retained until 1990. Martial law was finally suspended in 1983 but martial legislation continued to apply throughout the 1980s. For those living in Poland, the times were at the same time exciting and frightening: exciting because the Solidarity Movement was the first glimmer of hope for a besieged nation that was increasingly seeing itself as a 'Western country'. Wide access to television and slightly relaxed travel restrictions had shown them what they had always suspected: that the decadent ways of capitalism were not at all bad. But they were frightening times too: the iron fist of Soviet military force had already shown the citizens of Czechoslovakia and Hungary that errant nations could be very painfully brought into line.

The Poles were encouraged by the support – albeit tacit – they were receiving from the West: for example, Wałęsa was featured in many international media, notably on the cover of *Time*

Jean and Jan with Marysia, Robert, Michał and Dale, 1991

Magazine of January 4, 1982. In 1983 he was awarded the Nobel Peace Prize. But although released from prison and returning to his old job as an electrician at the Gdańsk Shipyard, he remained effectively under house arrest until 1987.

For ordinary people in Poland, life was little different: although restrictions began to be relaxed a little, food and other commodities were still scarce. Jean and Jan were now both retired and living on Jan's army pension. The government had always been reluctant to recognise those that had fought on the Western front whereas those that had fought alongside the Russians on the Eastern front were heroes. So it was a meagre pension but Wanda and Krysia were now independent and life was tolerable if not easy.

Wałęsa re-emerged in 1987 to organise and lead the semi-legal 'Temporary Executive Committee of Solidarity Trade Union', which led to the legalisation of Solidarity as a Trade Union. Two years later, he organised and led the Citizenship Committee of the Solidarity Trade Union. Formally, it was just an advisory body, but, in practice, it had become a political party.

All this now became world news: the destruction of the Berlin Wall; the Russian, Mikhail Gorbachev advocating *glasnost* and *perestroika*, and behind it all, the constant pressure from the Vatican and Pope John Paul II, the first Polish Pope. He had visited his native land in 1979 and thereby lit the fuse that was to detonate the explosion a decade later: the downfall of communism in Poland. At the end of 1989, the formerly Communist ally parties formed a non-Communist coalition government, which was the first non-communist government in the Soviet sphere of influence. After that agreement, to the surprise of the Communist Party, the parliament chose Tadeusz Mazowiecki as Prime Minister. Poland, while still a Communist country in theory, started to change its economy to a market base. At the end of that decade in 1989, Solidarity won a landslide victory, and a year later Lech Wałęsa became the President of Poland.

The Poles are nothing if not resilient: the way in which they preserved their language and culture after the Russians, Prussians, Austrians and Germans have at various times in their history annexed parts of the territory that is modern Poland, has been well documented. The country now turned its face to the West.

This had one very significant effect on Jan and Jean. Jan was now recognised for his war service in France, Holland and Germany, and was thus upgraded to full war veteran status; his pension was increased accordingly. It would be wrong to think that they were now showered with riches but at least they were able to live in greater comfort in their retirement.

16

Jan's Death

WITH THE ESTABLISHMENT OF SOLIDARITY and a democratic government in Poland, life took a different turn. Gone were the old Communist politicians, most of whom changed their suits and adopted a different ideology as if nothing had happened; gone were the hated UB; restrictions on religious practice were removed; freedom to travel was restored; people were allowed to own their own property and to run private businesses. The Poles are very good at private enterprise: indeed they had been honing their skills, black market trading and moonlighting for the last forty years under the Communists; it was just that it had to be under cover.

Krzysztof and Wanda took advantage of the relaxation of property restrictions to buy a plot of land on the edge of the forest about 70 kilometres outside Warsaw. Here they built a house with enough space for Wanda to create a substantial kitchen garden and for Krzysztof to use as a base for his fishing and wild boar shooting exploits. It is also home to a number of dogs they have acquired. Jean travels there with them frequently for weekends.

But there was another side to the coin. The changes mostly benefited young people: those that were socially and physically mobile, and not tied to dependents. As market forces were allowed to take hold, guaranteed full-time employment became a thing of the past; prices soared leaving pensioners and those on fixed incomes conspicuously worse off. There was plenty of food in the shops but not the money with which to buy it. So there was freedom but not prosperity. It would take another fourteen years and Poland's entry to the EU before that would happen.

For Jan and Jean the joys of the new Poland were tempered by the first signs of deterioration in Jan's health: he was beginning to show the first signs of Alzheimer's disease. Early symptoms were more irritating than worrying: inability to communicate, inability to react to situations and people, a slow withdrawal into silence. But Jean got an idea of how serious his condition had become when, one day when they were coming back from town on the tram, Jan got off unseen by her and disappeared for several hours before arriving home. He had, of course, no idea where he had been or indeed how he had found his way back.

After that and various other disturbing events around the home, Jean realised she could not ever again leave him alone. She was virtually confined to the house, having to be relieved by a minder every time she even needed to go to the market.

Jean and Krysia, 2007

Although Wanda and Krzysztof, Marysia and Michał all did what they could to help, they were all fully occupied in their own ways. Jan was slowly withdrawing from the world; this was a very exhausting and depressing time for Jean. She would play cards and children's games with him, feed him and dress him, but as the disease progressed and he became increasingly helpless and incontinent, it was like watching over the growth of a baby in reverse. To make matters worse, Alzheimer's sufferers, probably through frustration at their condition, frequently throw tantrums, which, because it is the behaviour of a baby conducted with the body and strength of an adult, can be terrifying. Jean needed all the self-reliance learnt in her childhood, the nursing skills from her training of sixty years earlier, the stoicism developed through years of hardship and the patience of a saint, to survive with her sanity intact.

Jean's flat, Kawcza, Warsaw, 2007

Wanda & Krzystof's country house at Łochów

Jan was, of course, under medical supervision, and at one stage he did go into hospital for a few days when Jean had become utterly exhausted, but he became so disturbed at being taken from his familiar surroundings – and she was so upset to see him in such a state – that she insisted on taking him home again, whatever the consequences. Jan died on 25 July 1998.

The funeral took place at Boremusza church and the veterans' association had ensured that it was carried out with full military honours. The coffin was brought into the church on a gun carriage with military escort. After the Requiem Mass it was taken to the family grave in Powązki Cemetery where Jan lies alongside his mother Stanisława, his brother Romek and his sister Jadzia, as were his wishes. Some months or years before – no one quite knows when – he had been to the grave and fixed the Polish army

45 Kawcza, Warsaw 2007

insignia to the headstone. A volley of shots was fired over the grave.

Here was an ironical twist: that recognition of Jan's wartime efforts, which had been studiously ignored by the regime for half a century, should be made after his death. How he would have enjoyed that ceremony!

And there was a further irony: after all the restrictions of movement under the communist regime and the more recent restraints caused by Jan's final illness, Jean was at last free to return to her beloved Scotland. But of course nearly sixty years of exile had built up its own bonds and way of life. She has her friends and three generations of family in Poland: life in 2007 Edinburgh would have been almost as strange as in 1947 Warsaw – and hideously expensive. Anyhow it is better to live with selected memories of childhood than to expose them to scrutiny in the reality of a different era.

Poland joined the EU in 2004 and prosperity there grows apace – even if they have some way to go before they learn how to govern themselves. After all, that is something they have not had much practice in lately. Shopping malls have sprung up, selling all the goods one would expect to find in Western Europe and attractive restaurants and cafes abound. Jean's grandson, Michał, who has followed his father as an airline pilot, was married recently in a style that would have been unthinkable even five years ago.

There is a spring in the step of young Poles nowadays. An enthusiasm for hard work, something that seemed pointless under communism, has been fanned into flame by the chance to earn real money. Many of them have grasped the opportunity to apply their skills in Western Europe, particularly Britain and Ireland, where their work ethic has earned them a good reputation, often putting the natives to shame. Some will stay in their country of adoption but many will return to Poland to enjoy their newly acquired wealth in a culture in which they feel comfortable.

This new wealth, one has to say, does not benefit pensioners who have seen prices rise alarmingly in recent years. However Jean has enough for her modest needs; any surplus she would give away anyhow! Her emotional attachment to Scotland remains strong and DVDs and videos of scenes of Scotland, its music and its dancing (sent by her brother, Ian) give her great pleasure – and she doesn't have to endure the Scottish weather.

Epilogue

A T THE TIME OF WRITING, Jean seems in good health and well placed to advance into her tenth decade. What are her thoughts as she looks back over this extraordinary life?

It is always difficult to be objective about one's own childhood, chiefly because, until later, there is nothing to compare it with. In Robbie Burns's words: "O wad some power the giftie gie us to see oursels as others see us!"

Her brother Ian has described well some of the attractions of a 'lighthouse childhood': the homes in varied, often beautiful places; the healthy outdoor life, the freedom to roam and endless opportunity for "messing about in boats". But there were disadvantages too: the isolation. It could be very lonely for a child, especially if there were no other children of a similar age among the lighthouse families. Moving every three years meant that there was nowhere to call home; it disrupted education and made friendships impossible to maintain. So the family was crucial and siblings are not always the best soulmates. At least in a family of five, Jean had some choice.

All three of the elder siblings have now passed away so I hope that a frank appraisal will not cause offence. Bessie was the 'leader of the pack', a strong woman who took it upon herself to be father's adjutant. She married Joe, a store man and dog breeder, lived in Musselbrough and had two children, Merle and John. Lena could be described as 'alternative' – rather a flashy dresser and a bit of a rebel; after the birth of June, she married Bill and had two more children, Douglas and Kenneth. Bert was altogether quieter – lacking in drive one might say – but he made a 'good' marriage to a prosperous fish merchant's daughter, although that developed into sadness later in life when his wife became alcoholic. The youngest, Ian, was the most obviously successful: after a stint in the Palestine police after the war, he joined the Metropolitan Police in London and then transferred to the Essex force, ending up as a Chief Inspector. He married Mary and they had two children, John and Susan.

Of the siblings, Jean was closest to Ian, although Bessie liked to pull the strings – certainly after father's death. But Jean, after her departure to Poland, was physically, culturally and emotionally separated from the rest of the family, so the relationships became ones of Christmas cards, occasional letters and even more occasional visits. The difficulties of day-to-day existence under the communist regime really overshadowed everything and preoccupation with survival was all consuming.

I am sure there are many other people that have overcome greater difficulties in their lives: refugees from war, starvation, torture and oppression, and those that have suffered from physical or mental illness or disability. However Jean's life has certainly been unusual. One is tempted to draw simplistic conclusions: to say that her ability to cope with hardship was forged in a childhood of harsh conditions; that her strength in adversity grew out of a strongly bonded family upbringing. Or one may take the American philosopher, Ralph Emersons's view that "what lies behind us and what lies before us are small matters compared to what lies within us". The reader will no doubt make his or her own judgement about a remarkable woman.